SLEEPING with GHOSTS!

A Ghost Hunter's Guide to Arizona's Haunted Hotels and Inns

by

Debe Branning

GOLDEN WEST ✪ PUBLISHERS

Dedication

To Franceska Mikova, my maternal grandmother and spirit guide who was as adventuresome as I am, and one of the first ghosts I had the pleasure to know.

Library of Congress Cataloging-in-Publication Data
Branning, Debe.
Sleeping with ghosts: a ghost hunter's guide to Arizona's haunted hotels and inns / by Debe Branning.
    p. cm.
Includes index.
ISBN 1-885590-97-0
1. Haunted hotels—Arizona. 2. Ghosts—Arizona. I. Title.
BF1474.5.B73 2004
133.1'09791—dc22   2004015706

Printed in the United States of America

2nd Printing © 2005

Copyright © 2004 by Debe Branning. All rights reserved. This book or any portion thereof, may not be reproduced in any form, except for review purposes, without the written permission of the author or publisher. Information in this book is deemed to be authentic and accurate by author and publisher. However, they disclaim any liability incurred in connection with the use of information appearing in this book.

Golden West Publishers
4113 N. Longview Ave.
Phoenix, AZ 85014, USA
(800) 658-5830

For entertaining excerpts and complete Table of Contents for all Golden West titles, visit: **goldenwestpublishers.com**

Table of Contents

Preface

Ghost-chasing has been a passion of mine for many years–before it was a popular thing to do. Ever since I was a little girl, I have been communicating with spirits. It was only natural for me to organize a ghost-hunting team that studies the paranormal. We have traveled to many historic locations in Arizona to learn *if* they are haunted, *why* they are haunted, and *who* may be doing the haunting. Our favorite adventures have been in Arizona's hotels, inns, and bed and breakfasts.

The public is fascinated with spirits, especially in the Southwest. One of the first questions asked by many travelers arriving at a hotel or bed and breakfast is, "Do you have a ghost?" Even when the answer is "Yes," most of the ghosts found in hotels are not frightening at all. There are no screaming skulls or chain-rattling spirits to keep you awake all night, and no monsters will snatch you up while you sleep. Even so, some haunted hotels are afraid that a ghost story or two will keep potential guests away. On the other hand, there are many haunted hotels that opt to promote their ghosts instead of keeping them secret or ignoring them. They honor their haunts like celebrities, and the entire staff treats them with utmost respect. It's no wonder that the most haunted rooms at these establishments are booked so often. If you don't immediately see or hear ghosts after checking in to a haunted hotel, don't despair; the odds are good that you will experience their pleasantly peculiar energies during your stay.

In my recent travels and studies, I have found the managers and innkeepers of these haunted places to be warm and friendly–always willing to give us a special tour of their establishment and share a few ghost stories along the way. Some tales are sad, some are mysterious and some are even humorous. The spirit world definitely has a sense of humor!

These haunted establishments are worth checking into, but remember when you do that you could be sharing a room with the spirit of someone who has never checked out!

Debe Branning

Foreword

The MVD Ghostchasers were established in 1995 when Debe Branning, Maureen Mustaca, Sherri Mintner and Toni Reed (all of whom worked, or have worked, for the Motor Vehicle Division in the Phoenix area!) packed their suitcases and headed for the haunted Gadsden Hotel in Douglas, Arizona. This first hotel proved to be the perfect spot for photographing spirits. Soon, other curious co-workers joined in our adventures and became a part of this motley bunch of paranormal investigators.

The MVD Ghostchasers have been dubbed the Scooby Doo entourage. Although we take ghost-hunting seriously, we are not afraid to make it fun. We always invite the spirits to interact with us, many times asking them to join us for the group photo. They almost always oblige us. Besides making the occasional house call, we also offer Spirit Photography Workshops for Arizona's paranormal investigators and beginning ghost hunters. The MVD Ghostchasers have held these workshops at old forts, abandoned cemeteries, haunted hotels, ghost mining towns, and bed and breakfasts, just to name a few. The guests attending the workshops have progressively grown in number and look forward to meeting every three months as they continue to develop their skills. In our attempts to determine who is doing the haunting and why, we have discovered just how rewarding the challenges of solving supernatural mysteries can be. This mission is not perilous, but it is exciting, and it has taken us to all corners of Arizona and many places in-between.

The success of this team is not due to any one person. Everyone contributes. Although none of us is what you would consider a psychic, some of us see spirits and some can hear them. Some can feel or smell them and others develop a bad headache or sick feeling in their stomachs when a ghost is near. There are even a few members who get a metal taste in their mouths, indicating a spirit's presence. But all of us *without exception* have experienced that cold chill followed by goose bumps. It is when we put all of our senses together that this paranormal team succeeds.

The MVD Ghostchasers have appeared on both local and international television, and many newspapers across the state have covered their investigations. This tiny group of ghostbusters has grown to become one of the top-notch paranormal teams in Arizona today.

MVD Ghostchasers

Debe Branning–director and founder of team
Lisa Maureen Mustaca–founding member
Sherri Mintner–founding member
Toni Reed–founding member
Liz Brown–Spanish interpreter
Roger Clark–senior member
Nancy Heath–a ghost-hunting granny
Maddie Herrick–workshop assistant
Denise Jordan–journal keeper and workshop assistant
Chris and Shiela McCurdy–we send them down to the dark, scary holes
Jo Skaggs–always ready for a new challenge
John Smith–debunker
Stu Sobrane–nerves of stone
Gary Tone–once a skeptic, now a believer
Nicole Wheeler–the youngest member, quite intuitive

Associate Members

Mark Christoph–photo debunker, historian
Becky Strong–Tucson partner
Megan Taylor–location interviewer

Rookie Investigators

Peggy Ebert
Diane and Mike Freeland
Steph Geerts

Mollie Hardesty
Beth Lister
Kenton Moore

Editor's Note:

While some orbs are clearly visible in photographs, others are barely discernible; we have added the "orb arrow" to the photographs in this book to help you spot and identify orbs.

Haunted Hotels and Inns Location Map

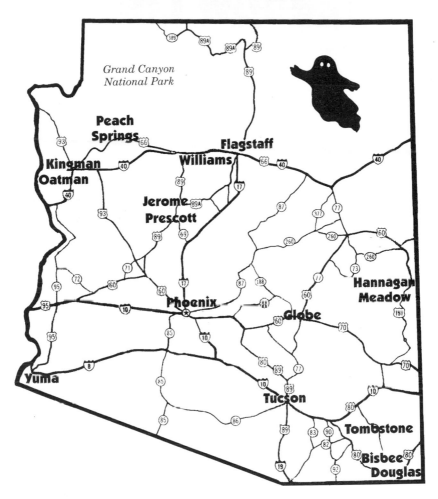

At the time *Sleeping with Ghosts* went to press, all the Hotels, Inns and Bed and Breakfasts mentioned were open and looking forward to your visit. As facilities and ownership change, please be sure to make advance reservations (addresses and phone numbers are listed at the end of each chapter).

Hannagan Meadow Lodge
Alpine

History

Both Hannagan Meadow Lodge and the meadow it is nestled in were named after Robert Hannagan. Originally a miner from Nevada who turned to cattle ranching during the 1870s, Hannagan moved to Arizona's White Mountains in the 1890s where he ran cattle between Alpine and "his" meadow for a living.

Hannagan Meadow Lodge was built in 1926 after the dedication of the Clifton to Springerville highway (once known as Route 666 and renamed Route 191) to provide a stopping place for travelers making the two-day trek through the mountains. Three governors and over 7,000 guests attended the event. In his dedication speech, Arizona Governor George W. P. Hunt baptized the route the "Coronado Trail," and the name stuck. It is believed to be one of the oldest roadways in

Arizona, and its history and breathtaking beauty have resulted in the route becoming a Scenic Federal Byway. It may even be the route traveled by Francisco Vasquez de Coronado and his armored caravan in 1540 as they traveled northward from Mexico in search of the mythical Seven Cities of Gold.

Owners Tom and Tessa Waite, with co-owners Larry and Traci Innes and managers Craig and Diane Service, continue Hannagan Meadow Lodge's proud legacy by preserving its history and maintaining its charm for future generations and guests. Throughout the years, various owners have made additions and improvements to the Lodge and surrounding property. The second and third floors, as well as the restaurant and cabins, were constructed in the 1950s. In 1996, everything was renovated so that all rooms and cabins were comfortable, rustic and delightfully cozy. Unique and relaxed, this mountain hideaway hosts many guests, including its famous resident ghost.

Ghosts

Several past owners of the Lodge have had encounters with the Lady of the Lodge. One such encounter occurred in the dead of winter (sometime between 1998 and 2000) when the lodge was supposed to be empty. It was a slow night, and no guests were registered. Mark Dauksavage, the previous co-owner, was locking up several of the outer buildings surrounding the main lodge after he had locked and shut off the lights of the main lodge itself. As he crossed the space between the lodge and general store, a light mysteriously turned on in the lodge's second floor hallway. Since no one was in the building, the light caught Mark's attention, and he paused, stopping to gaze up at the second floor window. What he was seeing was impossible: a young lady dressed in a white party dress was standing in front of the upper window, near the stairs, where there was no landing to stand upon (or any other kind of floor for that matter). Shocked, knowing that the building was empty, knowing that people cannot hover in mid-air, he ran to the only outside door and double-checked that it was still locked, and it was, just as he had left it. He fumbled for his keys, unbolted the double lock and raced madly up the only set of stairs in the building—stairs that should have put him face to face with the intruder. Mark found no one. Unable to accept that whoever it was could have escaped, he slowly began to check each room. The only way out of the building was the way he had come, so whoever he had seen was trapped and would have to pass by him in order to escape. His apprehension mounting, he came to the last room, gathered his courage and looked inside. It was empty. Puzzled and shaken, Mark turned around, scratching his head. There, at the other end of the hall, where he had initially seen the woman-in-white through the window, stood the beautiful young lady, waving a farewell to him as she gradually disappeared.

Carrie, Mark's wife, had maintained her office on the first floor, directly beneath that same window. She reported that when she was alone working late, she often heard footsteps leading to the window where the Lady of the Lodge had first appeared to her husband.

Lenora Price, granddaughter to previous owners Guy and Nora McCafferty, believes that the Lady of the Lodge is none other than her late grandmother after whom she was named, Nora Ellen Evans McCafferty. There is evidence to support this: the McCaffertys owned the Lodge from 1944-1969; a few years after they retired, Lenora's grandparents died, and paranormal phenomena began to occur in the Robert Hannagan Suite–a room that had once been the McCafferty's bedroom. Often, the door would swing open without cause, and lights would randomly switch on and off. As a way of memorializing her family's long association with Hannagan Meadow Lodge, Lenora presented management and staff with photos of her family and the Lodge itself in earlier days, contributing to the Lodge's ongoing effort to preserve and commemorate its history. Quite by coincidence–without knowing of the room's background–the decorator hung a portrait of her grandparents in the hallway facing the Hannagan Suite. Ghost activity in the room immediately ceased.

Lenora shared with me that Nora was a strong-spirited woman and a lover of nature who was able to communicate with wild animals, as well as someone who was both feared and revered. She knew about things before they happened and was not afraid to speak her mind. Lenora also described her grandmother as a woman ahead of her time, an advocate for many causes in her day. For instance, she rallied for a stoplight in Tucson, and her efforts resulted in the light being installed. As a willful woman who worked for what she loved and believed in, Nora McCafferty was the visionary and driving force behind many of the Lodge's improvements. She helped to make Hannagan Meadow Lodge a well-known tourist destination throughout Arizona, turning it from the run-down hunter's lodge it had been into a warm, family-friendly retreat.

It is no surprise, then, that Nora would continue to oversee this place she so cherished as the Lady of the Lodge. As long as she remains an owner of Hannagan Meadow Lodge in spirit, Nora's ghost will continue to watch over her special place in her own unique, mystical way. She was, and continues to be, the enduring force of the Lodge.

Address: HC 61 P.O. Box 335, Alpine, AZ 85920
Phone: 928-428-2225
Fax: 928-339-4702
Email: info@hannaganmeadow.com
Website: www.hannaganmeadow.com
Contact: Craig and Diane Service, managers
Lodging: 8 suites in Lodge; 10 rustic cabins
Amenities: private bath, buffet breakfast, fireplace

Bisbee
Grand Hotel
Bisbee

History

The Bisbee Grand Hotel was constructed in 1906 to provide lodging for traveling mining executives who came to Bisbee on business associated with the Phelps Dodge Copper Queen Mine. When the wooden structure burned down two years later in the fire that ravaged most of Bisbee's commercial district, the hotel was rebuilt along with the rest of the town, but this time, the hotel was constructed using cement (and its masonry work is impressive). It cost about $25,000 to rebuild–quite a tidy sum for its day. Instead of the rather plain hotel that it had been, however, the Bisbee Grand became an establishment of upscale structure and appearance, decorated in a traditional Western manner. The hotel's back bar fixture was transplanted from the Pony Saloon in Tombstone, Arizona, and dates back to the 1880s. A honky-tonk piano (an old style, tinny-sounding upright), also in the saloon, invites guests to play or sing along as someone else tickles the ivories.

The hotel received its current name when it was purchased in 1986. When Bill Thomas purchased the forsaken building early in 1999, he had it renovated and restored to its original, swank Old West Victorian style. The Bisbee Grand Hotel re-opened on July 1, 1999.

Ghosts

After being given keys to the rooms, the MVD Ghostchasers began to investigate the hotel, starting at the red-carpeted Grand staircase. (All of the guest rooms are located on the second floor and extend out from the stairs.)

The six team members split up, and each person selected a room to investigate. Within minutes, team member Nancy Heath called everyone over to the Oriental Suite. When I arrived, the light switch (which powered the fan as well) was off, and Nancy was standing in the dark. Once we were all in the room, the ceiling fan began to slowly turn itself clockwise; then it stalled, turned slowly once more, and finally, stopped moving completely. By the time I switched on the camcorder, all movement had ceased. This experience was followed by all of us feeling a cold presence pervading the room.

We believe that this ghost encounter may be linked to the authentic Chinese wedding bed in the room. It dates back to the 1890s, and spirits sometimes attach themselves to antiques—things from another era, like themselves.

Owner Bill Thomas has not seen the ghost who haunts the upstairs. However, at least eight different guests have. Known as the "Lady Ghost," she always appears to be the same age and wears the same color dress, with the same hair color and style, sometimes carrying a tea tray as well. She has been sighted in specific parts of the second floor with varying frequency: in the Victorian Suite; in the Cherub Room; in the Gray Room (Room 2); and in the northwest hallway.

Bill and his staff do not discuss the hotel's ghosts with visitors and adamantly refuse to divulge details of the Lady Ghost's appearance so that all ghost reports remain credible and unbiased. So when a guest claims to have seen a ghost, they are asked to relate their experience and describe what they saw without hints, prompting or other clues. Without exception, the color of her hair and dress does not change. Is it likely that such consistency is coincidental? Is it possible that people are somehow fabricating these identical details? The next four stories suggest that something beyond chance or imagination is at work. But the only way to know for sure is to investigate for yourself.

One of the most recent reports of the Lady Ghost came from a young boy. When the boy tried to convince his parents that he had seen a ghost, his parents insisted that he must have dreamed the experience. When Bill heard of the child's experience, however, he remained impartial; he asked the boy exactly what he had seen, and after the child described the ghost's dress and hair color, it was clear that she was a dead ringer for the Lady. Even though Bill suggested other colors to the boy that he might have seen, the child stuck by his version. Bill, impressed with the child's resolve, turned to the boy's parents and advised them not to discredit their son's claim about what he had seen because he had just described the Lady Ghost!

Another sighting involved a couple who had checked into the Victorian Suite. The woman, who was very intuitive, announced to her husband that she felt spirits in the room. Later, around 2:00 a.m., her husband awoke from a sound sleep and found a strange woman standing at the foot of the bed. (Seen in the moonlight, she appeared to be a living, breathing person, but when he described her to the hotel staff the next day, it became clear that he had witnessed the hotel's own Lady Ghost.) He lay motionless in bed for a few seconds with this strange woman standing in front of him. As he rose, she disappeared into the bathroom. When he proceeded to follow her inside, however, she was nowhere to be found!

During the restoration of the Grand, a drywaller also encountered this ghostly female. He had been working in the Gray Room when his partner announced it was time for lunch. As they were walking down the hallway, he felt the presence of someone behind him. Stopping at the head of the stairs to glance behind him, he saw a woman leaving the Bird Room (Room 3) and heading into the Gray Room. Since nobody was supposed to be in the hotel except the construction crew, he informed his partner that he was heading back to the room to tell the woman she needed to leave. When he entered Room 2, he was flabbergasted. The room was empty! His description of the woman also matched that of the Lady Ghost.

Sometime after the restoration was complete, a State of Arizona employee had an unnerving experience with a woman who fit the description of the Lady Ghost tucking him into bed. He even felt her dress brushing his arm hanging outside the covers. No sooner had he opened his eyes and spied her beside him than she vanished.

The management reports that there are always subtly mysterious things happening in the hotel but their spirits are friendly. It seems that the Lady Ghost has a counterpart, for downstairs there is a male ghost who likes to indulge in acts of innocent mischief. Bill shared one last ghostly story that still sends chills down his spine.

One evening, Bill was ousting a local street musician from the saloon because of drunken misbehavior. Bill began to tell the man that he could no longer listen to music in the saloon, and at that moment, a music box in the Lady's Lounge began to play. This music box had been broken for over four years. It continued to play for several seconds and has never played again! (Although he still banned him for the night, Bill maintained a friendship with the man and let him back into his establishment on a limited basis.)

While the street musician is no longer a regular, the ghosts are, so come prepared for an encounter with the unknown!

Address:	61 Main Street, P.O. Box 825, Bisbee, AZ 85603
Phone:	520-432-5900; Toll Free: 800-421-1909
Fax:	520-432-5900
Email:	BisbeeGrandHotel@msn.com
Website:	www.bisbeegrandhotel.com
Contact:	Bill Thomas, owner
Lodging:	theme rooms: 7 suites and 8 rooms, furnished with antiques and family heirlooms
Amenities:	full breakfast, TV, jacuzzi, fireplace, saloon

The Bisbee Inn
Bisbee

History

The Bisbee Inn was built in 1916 on the foundation of a wooden hotel that had burned to the ground during an intense fire. After its construction, Mrs. S.P. Bedford furnished and leased the two-story, red brick building to Mrs. Kate La More for $160 per month. In October of 1917, Hotel La More had its grand opening, functioning as a boarding house for copper miners and, arguably, as Bisbee's finest hotel. Three miners who each worked separate shifts would share a one-room living space and were provided with hot and cold water, wall sinks and a shared bathroom down the hall. Hotel La More was just up the hill from the train depot and even more convenient to the saloons and cribs of Brewery Gulch located a few paces away.

Mrs. Bedford took back the lease in the early 1920s but continued to operate the hotel under the La More name. From 1925 to 1936, Grace Waters owned and operated the establishment, changing its name to the Waters Hotel. During the 1940s, the hotel was converted into two-room apartments. It continued to function as an apartment building until the 1960s when JFK's newly created Peace Corps program transformed the building into a volunteer training center.

In 1982, the old hotel underwent a Certified Historic Restoration to become The Bisbee Inn. Its plumbing and wiring were replaced, the original woodwork was redone and skylights were added for the new atrium. The current owners, Moses and Brena Mercer, bought the Inn in May of 2003.

Ghosts

Kathleen Anderson, manager of The Bisbee Inn from 1996 to 2002, greeted the MVD Ghostchasers for our walk-through investigation. Escorting us through the atrium, she showed us where the ghost of a lady has been seen floating down the stairway wearing a flowing white gown and smelling sweetly of lilacs. She shared many ghost stories, several associated with the lady in white, including those she'd gathered over the years from the housekeeping staff.

Housekeepers have reported looking into a room moments after making up the beds to find them in complete disarray, unmade once again. Somehow, chairs and tables from guest rooms have wound up in the hallways as well. Although no one has seen how such things happen, unmade beds and migrating furniture have become an accepted part of working at the Inn.

While supernatural activity is common throughout the hotel, certain rooms seem to attract more ghosts than others. Rooms 12, 14, 15, 16, 17 and 23 have received the most ghost reports from guests and staff. For example, Room 23 has frequently been reported by guests to have a ghost cat. In Room 15, the imprint of a body sometimes appears on the bedding. Guests have reported resting on the mattress and feeling it sag with additional weight, as if someone was sitting or laying beside them. Room 12 is known for the soothing aroma of fresh lilacs.

The inexplicable lilac smell has also become linked to housekeeping's daily duties. Kathleen related a story about one of the housekeepers who had been having problems because she couldn't tolerate the odor of Clorox used throughout the inn to clean and sanitize. Although they tested several different Clorox fragrances, none of them masked the potent, underlying bleach scent. After a while, Kathleen noticed that the housekeeper was no longer complaining and inquired about the bleach's recent effect on her. The housekeeper explained that the horrible bleach smell had inexplicably changed into a fresh lilac scent, wiping out the disinfectant odor completely. These days, housekeepers expect something unusual to happen when they're cleaning and start to smell lilacs instead of bleach. They know the lady in white is near.

In 1958, the lady in white saved the lives of 3 children when she prevented them from exiting the back door seconds before a rock slide occurred on the back walkway. The children are grown and live in Bisbee today.

Another often-seen spirit is a tall man dressed in a vest with his jeans tucked into his boots. He has been sighted on the back stairs and appears to be a miner from the inn's boarding house era.

The Bisbee Inn offers more than just pleasing accommodations. It's a ghostly place where shadows move down hallways, doors slam for no apparent reason and the sound of clanging metal echoes through the corridors. The many cold spots that exist throughout the building hint at the numbers of ghosts within its walls. And there is always that flowery-fresh lilac scent that introduces the lady in white whenever she's near.

Address:	45 OK Street, P.O. Box 1855, Bisbee, AZ 85603
Phone:	520-432-5131; Toll Free: 888-432-5131
Fax	520-432-5343
Email:	BisbeeInn@aol.com
Website:	www.bisbeeinn.com and www.hotellamore.com
Contact:	Moses & Brena Mercer, owner/operators
Lodging:	20 rooms with private baths and phones with extra hook-ups for a modem
Amenities:	TV room, full complimentary breakfast in the dining room

Copper Queen Hotel

Bisbee

History

The Copper Queen Hotel was built in 1902, back when Bisbee was hailed as the world's largest copper mining town. Phelps Dodge Corporation funded the construction of the five-story brick hotel, both to provide lodging for potential investors they hoped to lure into their mining operations and to establish locations for essential local businesses, such as assay offices, brokerage firms and real estate developers. The Copper Queen also hosted other travelers, such as territorial governors and mining executives.

New York City architects Van Vleck and Goldsmith designed the hotel in an Italian Villa style, complete with high ceilings in each floor hallway and a traditional balcony on the third floor. It was built in the heart of the town at the bottom of Brewery Gulch, a district where all manner of entertaining pastimes–including seedy saloons and brothels–could be found. (Incidentally, if imitation is the sincerest form of flattery, then the exact replica of the Copper Queen constructed just a few years later in St. Augustine, Florida–the St. Augustine Hotel and Resort–is a tribute to the hotel's excellent design!)

In its heyday, the Copper Queen Hotel served as a social

center and meeting place for prominent guests and citizens alike, and it has remained a hub of activity. Famous guests include John Wayne and General John J. "Black Jack" Pershing, commander of the American Expeditionary Force in World War I. One of the most popular guest rooms is Room 211, John Wayne's former room, tucked away in a secluded corner on the second floor.

The hotel is home to antiques from Bisbee's boomtown era. Behind the front desk, for example, you can view the original switchboard and hotel safe. Adjacent to the lobby, visit the award-winning Copper Queen Saloon, just to watch the unique local personalities if nothing else. And be sure to climb the original staircase that leads to the second floor. If you do venture upstairs (or anywhere else for that matter), watch for ghosts, too.

Ghosts

The Copper Queen Hotel is one of the most talked about haunted hotels in Arizona. And the most talked about spirit in the hotel is Miss Julia Lowell, a prostitute who is believed to have worked here for a number of years in the early 1900s. It is said that Julia took her life when a gentleman she fell in love with spurned her, deciding he wanted nothing to do (romantically speaking) with a scarlet lady. She was in her early 30s when she died. Although she used several rooms in the Copper Queen to ply her trade, Room 315 was named in honor of her and is believed to have been one of the rooms in her favored working area. Her presence is most commonly felt on the west side of the building, on the third floor.

It is not unusual for Julia to favor those she likes with her attentions. But she only appears to men. Some "lucky" men hear a female voice whispering in their ear. While she sometimes materializes as bright white smoke, she has also been seen as a very real-looking woman, barely dressed, posing on the grand stairway clutching a bottle of "spirits."

Several gentlemen guests have had the pleasure of Miss Lowell's company after checking into Room 315. After waking up all of a sudden, for no apparent reason, they have sat up in the middle of the night to find the middle-aged former stripper and dancer performing for them, dancing her seductive striptease near the foot of the bed. When they reached out to touch her, she just smiled and faded away. Many think the lady they see on the stairs wearing a long black dress is also Julia, in a different guise.

There is a ghost of a young boy who frolics on the third floor. His mother evidently worked in the hotel dining room, and he spent his days playing inside and outside the massive hotel. Some say that he drowned in a neighboring pond. Legends say that he was about 8 or 9 years old when he drowned in the San Pedro River. Presumably, his spirit found its way back to the hotel because his mother was here.

Manager Scott Smith told the MVD Ghostchasers about the following incident he witnessed in the dining room: A family was having breakfast together when their young daughter became interested in something underneath the next table. She began to fidget and tried to climb down from her seat, telling her parents that she wanted to go play with the little boy. Her parents looked around the room and saw no one. "What little boy?" they asked as she crouched down to the floor. "The little boy under the table!" the young girl pointed. There was no boy in sight.

This pint-sized ghost apparently likes to play pranks on guests by hiding various objects in the room from them. Some say that when they run bath water, they can hear him crying.

The third prominent ghost in the Copper Queen is an older gentleman dressed in a fine black suit, usually seen in the stairway and lobby area. He is tall, with long hair and beard, usually seen wearing a black cape and top hat. Some claim they smell the odor of a cigar before or after seeing him. He usually appears in doorways or as a shadow in the rooms on the fourth floor's southeast corner. One guest witnessed him stepping *through* the closed elevator doors. He had looked like an ordinary man until he disappeared.

Scott Smith took us up to a penthouse without public access and explained why it was no longer the location of his office. He had wanted his office to be in this small attic penthouse when he first became manager of the Copper

Queen because of the view. He set up his desk and computer in front of one of the windows. Each morning he came upstairs and unlocked the door. And each morning, he would find his chair in the corner, toppled over as if someone had thrown it across the room. This happened several times, until Scott got the message that "someone" did not want him in the room. He decided to move his office to a lower level.

The third floor seems to be the most active floor (and not just because of Julia). Rooms 304 and 308 have doors that open and shut on their own. A male apparition in Room 312 likes to move guests' belongings around the room. He is impish in character and wears a hat. Two women staying in Room 312 reported a hat materializing out of thin air. It floated around the room, sailing slowly before their eyes, until all of a sudden, it vanished. Others staying here have heard the tinkling of bells. Guests in Room 309 often feel a cold presence. A manager once saw ectoplasm when he walked through the door. When he reached out to touch the strange substance, he found it was cold.

Many guests report a strong wind inside Room 212 that shakes the doors and windows through the night.

A night porter witnessed a light that seemed to emerge from one of the large mirrors in the lobby. The orb moved around the room, floated up the staircase and vanished.

The spirits in the Copper Queen Hotel enjoy mingling with the living guests, and they get even more lively when the hotel hosts its interactive weekend murder mystery game, "The Ghost of the Copper Queen." The game may be make-believe, but the ghosts are real.

Address: 11 Howell Ave., Drawer CQ, Bisbee, AZ 85603
Phone: 520-432-2216
Fax: 520-432-4298
Email: info@copperqueen.com
Website: www.copperqueen.com/hotel
Contact: Tracy Glover, general manager
Lodging: 48 rooms
Amenities: AC, TV, direct-dial phones, swimming pool, Old West Saloon, restaurant, mezzanine, fireplace

The Inn at Castle Rock
Bisbee

History

An artesian spring once bubbled at the base of Castle Rock, the most prominent landmark in Bisbee. In 1877, Sergeant Jack Dunn stopped underneath the rock formation for water and found there were traces of silver in the canyon. Soon after, he staked his claim here, and before long there were hordes of miners digging and staking claims, forming the mining camp that grew into the town of Bisbee. Eventually, the overzealous miners dug a silver shaft too close to the spring, causing the water to breach the thin barrier and flood the shaft. As you would expect, the mine was abandoned, but as you might not expect, the spring (by this time called Apache Spring) was capped off and made into the town well, which supplied Bisbee with water for a number of years.

Bisbee's first mayor, a man by the name of Joseph Muirhead, built a boarding house for miners on this site in 1895. The building was converted into apartments in the 1950s and became a Bed and Breakfast in 1982 when the late

Jim Babcock acquired the property and began tending to its metamorphosis. He owned and managed the Inn at Castle Rock for many years, using his creativity and hands to make his dreams for the sanctuary come true. Affectionately known as the "Wizard of Castle Rock," he was regarded as a spiritual leader in the community, a man with a magical way about him. Jim's daughter, Jeannene Babcock, assumed ownership in 1997 after her father passed away.

Today the Inn at Castle Rock is an impressive sight as you wind your way down Tombstone Canyon. Nestled in the canyon among several other buildings, it is a colorful, mostly red, three-story Victorian building with cream-colored wrap-around balconies. The acre of gardens behind the Inn (planted by the Wizard) contains all manner of flowers and greenery, including fruit trees, English-Algerian ivy, wild flowers and larkspur, along with an assortment of other plants that attract hummingbirds.

Inside, all of the rooms are different. Antiques accent each room's eclectic decor; for instance, one room's walls are covered in maps, and another room's ceiling is overlaid with East Indian batiks. Beds come in all varieties: brass, wooden and iron, covered with country quilts and bedspreads featuring Native American designs.

Breakfast in the Eccentricity Dining Room provides a delightful start to the day. These days, this is where Bisbee's former water source can be found. When Jim Babcock bought the Inn, the once-essential well was just a hole in the dirt covered with boards. He converted it into a fishpond where Japanese koi now frolic.

Ghosts

The staff of the Inn at Castle Rock did not promise us any spirit activity. But when the MVD Ghostchasers make a call, you never know what will happen.

The desk clerk told us we could roam freely in the Inn but to please stay off the fourth floor, where the private living quarters are located. We could feel Babcock's presence throughout the Inn as we explored the unoccupied rooms.

As ghost hunter Peggy Ebert was sitting on the staircase that led to the fourth floor, she felt a chill run through her body. She stood up, and I snapped a picture. In the middle of the steps, there was an orb seeming to act as a sentry, guarding the entrance to the private, "off-limits" area. We have always felt it was the Wizard protecting his home.

Staff and guests have reported feeling a consistent, very uncomfortable sensation in what is called the Tasmania Room. They describe it as a feeling of being watched.

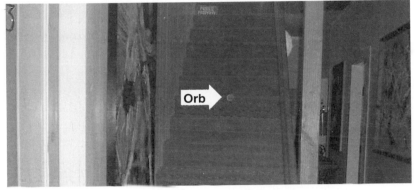

The sentry of the Inn at Castle Rock "on duty."

Legend has it that a man in a room facing the street was cleaning a gun when it accidentally discharged, fatally wounding a woman across the street. Perhaps her spirit stays here, searching the Inn for the source of her untimely death.

The spiritual energy of the Wizard is felt especially in the gardens and art gallery. His presence is a protective reassurance to his daughter, innkeeper Jeannene.

Address:	112 Tombstone Canyon Rd., Bisbee, AZ 85603
Phone:	520-432-4449 or 520-432-7195
	Toll Free: 800-566-4449
Fax:	520-432-7868
Website:	www.theinn.org
Email:	mail@theinn.org
Contact:	Jeannene Babcock, innkeeper
Lodging:	15 rooms with private baths
Amenities:	fireplace, gardens, outdoor patio, art gallery and breakfast, pets welcome

OK Street Jailhouse Inn

Bisbee

History

This two-story building on OK Street was built in 1904 as the local branch of the Cochise County Jail, just one block from Bisbee's famous Brewery Gulch where wild saloons catered to miners. But by 1915, during Bisbee's mining boom, the jail was unable to handle the weekend overflow of prisoners; the drunk tank packed as many men behind bars as possible so that the cellblock quite literally became a sweatbox. When a larger detention facility was built nearby, the OK Street Jailhouse was closed. For decades, it sat vacant.

During the 1950s, when Bisbee was often used as a filming location for Westerns, John Wayne had part ownership in the jailhouse. In 1988, the jail was converted into a two level suite and has captured the hearts of travelers ever since.

The jailer's office now serves as a small sitting room. The old drunk tank downstairs was converted into a modern living room with a sofa bed, and the cell that held the jail's most serious criminals is the new upstairs bedroom suite. There is a closet in the corner where the solitary confinement cell was located. You can stay for a weekend getaway, or you can opt to serve some serious time behind bars and stay as long as your vacation allows. Whatever you decide, make your reservations in advance. Modern decor against the original steel bars create the perfect mood for a weekend escape.

Ghosts

The MVD Ghostchasers visited the jailhouse to investigate possible paranormal activity. "Inmate guests" Debbie and Neil welcomed us into their weekend retreat to see if any spirits were lingering.

We captured several pictures of orbs, the prisoners seeming to peer from behind the steel bars. Debbie later confirmed this finding, sharing that she has felt someone watching her while reading or working on her computer.

When guests arrive, they often ask "jailer" Doris Turner if their "confined quarters" are haunted. Doris promptly shows her inmates the orb photos from our investigation and informs them that there is a distinct possibility they will have some additional cellmates during the night.

The steel bars cast eerie shadows as the afternoon turns to night. These shadows once fell over drunks and violent criminals, making today's "inmates" thankful they have the keys to their cellblock. It appears that even though their jail sentences are over, many of the former cons are not taking advantage of parole in the afterlife. Come see how comfortable being behind bars can be. Consort with old-time desperadoes and live to tell about it!

Address:	9 OK Street, P.O. Box 1152, Bisbee, AZ 85603
Phone:	520-432-7435; Toll Free: 800-821-0678
Fax:	520-432-7434
Email:	doris@okrealtyinc.com
Website:	www.okrealtyinc.com
Contact:	Doris or Reg Turner, jailers/property managers
Lodging:	1 suite
Amenities:	TV, phone, kitchenette, jacuzzi and 2 sitting rooms, small pets welcome

Oliver House
Bisbee

History

The Oliver House is perched high on a slope that overlooks Main Street in downtown Bisbee. The path leading up to the two-story, red brick Bed and Breakfast meanders along, stretching over a canal, where it briefly becomes a footbridge, and resumes as a footpath until it reaches its destination. The building was constructed in 1908 as an upscale boarding house for mining executives, and later harbored miners as well. Edith Ann Oliver named the building after her husband, Henry, who made his fortune in mining.

The house looks much like it must have in 1908. The hardwood floors shine. Sunlight pours in through the original glass windows. Both floors have broad hallways. Every sound creates an echo magnified by the 10-foot-high ceilings. The rustic, Western Victorian look of the Oliver House complements its stately character and compelling past.

Like many other boarding houses of its time, the Oliver House's history includes violent shootings dating back to the 1920s. It is said that twenty-seven people have died here since the house's construction.

Patty Hill purchased the Bed and Breakfast in May 2003, taking on the ghosts that her predecessor Dennis Schranz initially scoffed at.

Ghosts

Former owner Dennis Schranz purchased the neglected house in 1986 despite the rumors he had heard about the place. Dennis ignored the former owners' stories about the five ghosts who supposedly resided in the house. Then he spent a night here.

Right away there were unnatural occurrences, but they were minor, it seemed, and easy enough to dismiss. While moving in, for instance, his puppy tugged against the leash, pulling away from the front door, and refused to enter. Dennis carried the pup inside instead, and the terrified creature promptly hid underneath the nearest piece of furniture. Chalking the behavior up to adjustment jitters, he went about his business until he finally climbed into bed, ready for a good night's sleep. But during the course of the first night, Dennis began hearing unsettling noises.

Dennis was unable to ignore the sounds of running water, footsteps and creaking hinges echoing around him—noises that continue to recur throughout the house. Cold spots arise frequently here, too. At one point while Dennis lived here, the ghost activity became so intense that he had the home blessed by a Catholic priest. This seemed to calm the spirits for a time; the intensity of the hauntings temporarily subsided.

Once, Dennis stood in the center of the living room and had a talk with the ghosts. He told them that he lived here now and they would all have to work together. Dennis' declaration seemed to do the trick. The activity decreased immensely. In effect, he showed the spirits that he did not fear them, and they responded by respecting his strength.

Room 13 is reportedly the most ghost-active room in the entire Oliver House. The room may have belonged to Nat Anderson, a mining company employee who was shot on February 22, 1920, at the top of the stairway. Rumors say that Nat's murderer had two possible motives for shooting him: Nat owed the man money, and Nat was having an affair with the man's lady. This unfortunate soul was shot in the forehead, chest and back. His murder has never been solved.

Another story stems from the Blue Room, the site of a

violent confrontation in 1932 that resulted in the deaths of three people after a local policeman caught his wife in bed with another man. He shot them both dead where they lay. Then he turned the gun on himself.

Violent acts of retaliation are not the only events that may have given rise to the Oliver House's ghosts. "Grandma" was an elderly lady who died of natural causes while living here; she has apparently chosen to stay on in the Oliver House as a ghostly resident. Guests report that at 2:00 a.m. a cold breeze flows through Grandma's Room. The cold breeze that announces her presence coincides with the timing of two other spooky occurrences. Visitors have noted that the room's ceramic cuckoo clock cuckoos at 2:00 a.m., even though it has no clockworks. Also around 2:00 a.m., Grandma is seen rocking in the rocking chair. Perhaps 2:00 a.m. is the token time of her death?

On the Saturday afternoon that the MVD Ghostchasers visited the Oliver House, we were warmly greeted by the housekeeper who gave us our grand tour. She promptly took us into the kitchen to read some of the newspaper clippings that featured the haunting of Oliver House. Afterwards, the group was ready to go upstairs and check the paranormal

Team member Nancy in the Oliver House's Pink Room with someone watching over her!

activity in the guest rooms. Everyone had left the room except team members Peggy Ebert, Gary Tone and me when we met one of the Inn's ghosts. Suddenly, without anyone touching the kitchen door, the door began to slowly swing shut, giving us the distinct impression that "someone" was closing it. After waiting a few minutes, we reopened the door that divided the kitchen from the hall and took pictures from both sides of the door.

The housekeeper permitted us to go upstairs and photograph the rooms. After snapping many orb shots in the rooms and main hallway, we entered Room 13 where we all felt a sad, sick feeling. Two very large orbs showed up around several team members who had gathered to discuss their photos. Could they have been the spirits of two miners who continuously pace the halls of the Oliver House? And are these the same pranksters who open and close the doors in the Purple Sage Room?

As we gathered downstairs to thank the housekeeper for letting us conduct our investigation, the kitchen door once again began to slowly close before our eyes. We chose to view this act as the spirits waving us goodbye!

Address:	26 Sowles Road, Bisbee, AZ 85603
Phone:	520-432-1900
Email:	oliverhouse@theriver.com
Contact:	Patty Hill, owner/innkeeper
Lodging:	12 rooms: some with private baths and some with shared
Amenities:	living room, dining room, phone, breakfast, full-length porch, gardens

Gadsden Hotel
Douglas

History

Located one mile north of the Mexican border, the Gadsden Hotel in Douglas is a fine establishment that has definitely earned its reputation as "The Last of the Grand Hotels." Architect Henry Trost, famous for his Southwest building designs, is responsible for the hotel's elaborate architecture. Completed in 1907, the Gadsden is both classic and elegant, featuring a lobby with vaulted stained-glass skylights and a curving, solid white Italian faux marble staircase. Floor-to-ceiling marble pillars covered in 14-karat gold leaf accent the decor, and the mezzanine features a Tiffany stained-glass mural that extends forty-two feet across an entire wall. A large, well-known painting titled "In the Western Desert" by Audley Dean Nicols, an early 20th century artist famous for his desert landscape depictions, hangs just below the window.

The hotel was named after the Gadsden Purchase of 1853, which granted Mexico's territory south of the Gila River—an area roughly the size of Pennsylvania—to the United States. Its grand opening was a momentous occasion in Douglas, and everyone attended the gala event. Prominent ranchers, cattlemen, bankers and business owners went inside to celebrate while the rest of the townspeople stood in the street near the entrance, marveling at the ball gowns and listening to the music. The fancy hotel inevitably became the focal point for club and civic group meetings.

In 1928, a terrible fire destroyed the Gadsden, burning the building to its foundations but claiming no lives in the process. Determined to make it fire resistant, it was reconstructed using structural steel and reinforced concrete—again according to the Trost design—on the foundation of the original building. Only this time, the hotel's orientation was shifted so that the Gadsden's main entrance was facing G Avenue, the town's new main street, instead of 11th Street, Douglas' former main drag. The marble staircase was pulled from the basement and reset in its place of grandeur. No cost was spared in the building's reconstruction. It featured the finest materials and fixtures, including a plumbing system with copper pipes. This second Gadsden Hotel took almost two years to complete.

Legend has it that the famous Mexican bandit and revolutionary Pancho Villa rode his horse up the lobby's marble staircase sometime before the fire of 1928. Apparently, during the course of this arrogant display, one of his horse's hooves left a nasty chip in the marble that can still be seen on the seventh step (or pointed out by hotel staff with an explanation about why the event is a likelihood, not a legend).

Almost every governor of Arizona has stayed in the Gadsden. Many noteworthy celebrities have stayed here as well, including: Eleanor Roosevelt, evangelist Amie Semple McPherson, and actors Alan Ladd, Paul Newman, Charlie Sheen and Tom Selleck.

The five-story structure was placed on the National Register of Historic Places in 1976. When the Brekhus family purchased the hotel in 1988, they began to restore it to its original condition. Their ongoing restoration efforts have returned the Gadsden Hotel to its former glory so that it is once again Douglas' most popular gathering place, tourist attraction and landmark.

Ghosts

The Gadsden Hotel is a treasure chest of ghosts! The MVD Ghostchasers have been visiting the hotel on a regular basis for the past several years—so often that the hotel staff recognizes us as soon as we walk in the door. They're always eager to divulge their latest ghost sightings, and they even know which rooms we prefer to stay in on the second floor (in the area we like to think of as "our special wing").

Starting from the top—the fourth floor—I'll unravel the ghost stories as we descend. The fourth floor is accented in red, which always reminds us of passages from Stephen King's book *The Shining* about the red in the Overlook Hotel's hallways. This association between the Gadsden Hotel and *The Shining's* Overlook Hotel is a little spooky because of the horror caused by the poltergeists in King's make-believe hotel. When I'm walking down the fourth floor's red hallways late at night, the "red rum" chant (*murder* spelled backward) pops into my head, and it's hard to shake. It makes me wonder what dark mysteries this hotel contains.

While most of the hotel's ghost activity takes place in the southwest corner of the building, the entire fourth floor is an extremely haunted area. This makes the fourth floor's southwest corridor perhaps the most haunted area of the entire building. You can test out this claim for yourself and make up your own mind about it, but the stories that follow make a good case that it's true.

After delivering a message to a guest on the fourth floor, one of the elevator operators was on his way back to the elevator when he saw the shadowy image of a tall man standing in the southwest corner. The ghost frightened him so much that he ran backwards all the way to the elevator, afraid to turn his back on the unknown. We have seen an apparition of a tall man standing in the right corner that resembles photographs of Pancho Villa and believe it is the same spirit the elevator operator witnessed. We have filmed large orbs in this hall as well (see photo next page).

When Ghostchaser team member Jo and I investigated this area, we felt nothing in the corner itself but did feel eyes

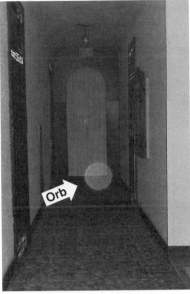

Ghost "dead" ahead.

watching us from down the hall. As we walked down the hallway, halfway down we walked into a large cold spot. Both of us felt the familiar presence of the ghost we had nicknamed Sara (the name she'd given us via our spirit board), and we asked Sara if we could take her picture. That's when amazing phenomena began to happen. Not about to miss this chance for such great footage, Jo began snapping pictures, and I started filming with my camcorder. Small pink dots of light began to move down the wall. As the dots passed over the black doors, their color was changing to blue. We must have followed these mutating dots fifteen feet before they finally settled in a corner.

Where's Sara?
She's in the window frame!

Although Jo took the shot, the dots didn't show up in the photo. In the very last photo Jo snapped, as I was pointing at a blue orb, we saw an apparition of Sara's face in the wood paneling of the southwest corner window frame.

Sara also made an appearance when I was staying in Room 437. Sometime around 1:30 a.m., someone in the hallway tried to open the door. Initially, when I heard the key being inserted into the lock, it startled me. So I hopped out of bed in a hurry, yelling, "There's somebody in here!" The voice on the other side responded softly, "There must be some kind of mistake."

Rubbing sleep from my eyes, I opened the door to see a small, fluorescent, white-haired lady standing before me who was not the least bit threatening. Feeling strangely reassured and peaceful–almost like my grandmother had been checking up on me–I closed the door, crawled back into bed and fell asleep. The next day, I figured out that my late-night encounter had been with a ghost!

Just down the hall in Room 433, there is a gentleman ghost who pushes the chair away from the desk. Whenever someone enters the room, the chair is pulled out as if someone else is sitting in it. He also occasionally calls out the name of whomever is currently sharing the room with him.

One humid evening, team member Maureen escorted her son, Garrett, and my daughter, Nicole, to Room 433. Since the room was being painted, they weren't surprised when they found the door unlocked. Despite the desert heat outside, one of the telltale signs of spirit activity was present: It was extremely cold in the room–one huge cold spot. The room was bare due to the remodeling, and the bed was stripped and TV removed–nothing unusual there–but the chair was pulled away from the desk as if someone was sitting in it, watching them. None of the three could shake the feeling of being watched. (And if that doesn't seem spooky, maybe you should check out the room for yourself!)

For a peaceful night's sleep, the third floor is the floor you must request. We have not heard of many ghost tales occurring on this level, known as the Green floor.

The second, or Pink, floor is a different case. We prefer to stay on this floor in the south corridor because of all the amazing ghost encounters we have had in this area. In our experience, the most haunted room in this hallway is Room 245. We call it the Pancho Villa Room as a result of a fateful experience we had in it some years ago.

In November 1996, team member Gary (who *always* stays in this room) had the pleasure of sharing Room 245 with Pancho Villa's ghost for twenty-four hours. All day, the aroma of stale, musky men's cologne grew stronger and stronger in the room. Gary opened the windows to air it out, but the stench remained. At some point later in the evening, the girls in the adjoining room heard a man singing what sounded like a bit of opera. Assuming it was Gary, they teased him about his impromptu "performance," but Gary had been watching a karate movie all evening. He declared himself innocent.

Even though he received no formal education, we know from our research that Pancho Villa loved poetics and word games. He found them amusing, and they made him seem well-educated even though he was basically illiterate. Partly because he wanted to be able to entertain heads of state, he would hire teachers to come into his home and educate him in verse and literature. This background information is necessary in order to understand our amazement at what happened next in Room 245.

Later that night, we talked Gary into using the spirit board with us. We started our session by asking if Pancho was in the room. The planchette indicated, "Yes," and then countered with the question, "R U G T?" which we understood to mean, "Are you Gary Tone?" When we asked Pancho to name his legitimate wife, the planchette slowly spelled "M-A-R-I-A," which was correct.

Thinking he smelled a rat, Gary assumed that we were just tricking him, manipulating the board ourselves. In order to test who was really moving the planchette, he asked, in Spanish, the name of Pancho's favorite horse. The answer came back, "S H T." At that point, we all became confused. After returning home and doing some research, though, we found information that indicated we really did communicate with Pancho Villa's spirit through the spirit board. Pancho's favorite horse's name was Seven Leagues, or Siete Leguas in Spanish. Pancho's spirit had been telling us the answer in Spanish phonics. "S II T" was actually indicating the Spanish word for seven—*siete* (si e te)—broken down into phonics. This response was a clever demonstration of Pancho's ongoing love for games involving wordplay.

Room 245 also has a closet full of hangers that swing back and forth intermittently. While investigating, team members Gary Tone and Stu Sobrane have both been locked in the room's bathroom. To this day, Stu swears that someone pushed him in the shower and it wasn't Gary. Some ghosts definitely have a sense of humor.

During another visit to the hotel in January of 1997, the door to Room 202 would not open to any adult. Whenever one of the team members tried to unlock the door, it was as if we were using the wrong key for the lock. We were only able to get into the room when one of the teens used the key (the *same* key); for them, it turned inside the lock without any problem. Whenever the key was placed on the dresser, it would disappear again when someone was attempting to leave the room. After a search, one of the teenagers would inevitably find the key in its original spot on the dresser. Morever, clothes and towels would not stay hung up in the bathroom. They would wind up on the floor no matter how well they had been secured above it.

While staying in Room 206, team member Sherri arranged her clothes on the bed and stepped into the shower. After toweling off, she discovered that her socks were missing from the pile. They were never found. On another occasion when Jo and I were sharing Room 206, her makeup bag turned up missing. One moment it was there, and the next, it was gone.

The ghost of a tall man haunts the laundry room on this floor from time to time as well. His spirit has been seen running from the room, as if he is chasing someone. Team member Nicole always gets spooked when she is near the laundry area because she feels like someone is watching her from inside the room; not surprisingly, she refuses to enter this room alone. Most people—everyone on the team, in fact—report feeling a sense of despair or unhappiness here.

At one time, the ghost of a girl we called Allison lingered in the halls of the second floor, lost and searching for her family. We contacted a channeler who removed her from the bonds of the hotel and sent her spirit home to her loved ones. Before Allison departed, the channeler was able to determine that Allison and her family had stayed on the second floor, but Allison became seriously ill and died at a later point on their journey. Only a small child when she died, Allison's spirit had wandered back to the hotel, looking for her mother in the last place she had been healthy and happy while alive.

We tend to spend a lot of time on the mezzanine. This is where we encountered the ghost of the ten-year-old Native American boy named Nazanaza (affectionately tagged "Naza" by the group). We had heard many tales of the "wild child" who played pranks on the guests in the mezzanine area. His mischief includes flicking lights on and off, knocking over items in various rooms and hiding things from guests.

Chris McCurdy surrounded by two large orbs on the mezzanine.

Our first encounter with Naza was the night of the Douglas Annual Christmas Light Parade. As we were sitting in the southwest corner of the mezzanine using the spirit board, we could feel the presence of a young boy around us, so we asked the spirit his name and age. He responded by communicating through the board that he was ten years old and named Nazanaza. Through the course of the evening, he used the board to reveal that he had died in 1919 after sneaking into the Gadsden to see the Christmas tree. When hotel personnel spotted him, they chased him through the mezzanine, trying to roust him from the building. Running away from them at full tilt, he fell over the edge of the rail to his death in the lobby below.

When he concluded his tragic story, we asked if he would show himself to us. Within moments, a shadow appeared on the wall. Nicole stood up to see if she could feel his presence, and at that moment, a cold breeze rushed through Gary's right arm and up the back of his neck, knocking the breath right out of him. Naza's ghost had run *through* him, producing what felt like an electrical shock!

During a New Year's weekend at the Gadsden, Nazanaza appeared to team members Nancy, Maureen and me while we were there for a three-day stint investigating and hoping for a sighting. It was Sunday morning, and we were about to leave when something truly magical happened. Maureen noticed an aqua-blue dot on the floor, about six inches in diameter, so bright it was almost fluorescent. It would fade out and reappear a few inches away from its previous spot. Mesmerized, we followed the moving circle of light for about six feet. Then, to test its response, I moved directly in front of it and promptly stopped. It stopped. I took three steps backward, and it backtracked with me. I stopped again, but this time a cold breeze flew past my shoulder and over the mezzanine. Unfortunately, none of us had taken our cameras with us to record this large, migrating, aqua-blue dot, and it vanished with the breeze.

Nicole actually saw young Naza's ghost on one visit. He had communicated to her via the spirit board that he would appear for her, but *only* to her (they have quite a bond). While Nicole was relaxing in one of the lobby's comfortable chairs, she looked up and saw what appeared to be a boy walking along the mezzanine, with long black hair and wearing a black shirt. Jumping up all of a sudden, she shouted, "Oh my God! I just saw him!" She pointed to the north side of the mezzanine where she saw him walk across the room, go behind a pillar and disappear.

Since about 1997, we have been bringing gifts for Naza to find. He has requested that we hide our trinkets in the plants for him. We have complied with his wish, and when we return to the plant later, the gift is gone (quickly whisked away like any child's present). We started this tradition by first leaving him a wooden pig. Another time, we hid a small teddy bear in the plant, waited to see how he would claim it and saw the leaves move as if he was looking through the plant for the bear. We brought him candy corn once but learned ghosts just don't like sweets like we do. He left that present in the plant!

We have also played jacks with him (rather unsuccessfully) and blown bubbles to amuse him. When blowing bubbles, we have watched them float down, at which point Naza pops them one by one, and observed others drift down and rise back up again, like Naza is blowing them into the air again before popping them.

Our experiences with Gadsden ghosts do not end with Nazanaza. Jo once had a psychic flash in the Kopper Room, one of the Gadsden's banquet rooms, also located on the mezzanine. After walking into the darkened room, a vision suddenly appeared before her eyes. A blond lady in a red flapper dress was standing behind a casino gambling table, holding a drink in one hand and a cigarette in the other. She was arguing with a round, bald-headed man. They were both standing near a window through which the town's lights were visible. Then, as suddenly as it had begun, the room returned to normal–vacant and windowless–leaving Jo disoriented and confused. Later, during another renovation, drywall was removed from the walls, and the hidden windows were discovered, located in exactly the same place that Jo had seen them in her vision. Somehow, when she entered the room, Jo had been transported back to another date in time and had glimpsed an incident that had occurred in the room long ago.

After hours party for one in the Kopper Room!

It is rumored that Pancho Villa's ghost still roams the basement in search of his decapitated head. If you don't know how his head was decapitated, allow me to briefly explain. Pancho was buried in 1923 after being assassinated with his head intact. Later in the 1920s, it was all the rage with the East Coast Ivy Leaguers to showcase the skull of a famous person in their frat houses. A man was allegedly hired to steal Pancho's head for one of these fraternities, and one of the Gadsden's former owners was an alleged acquaintance of the man paid to steal the head. Although this owner pretended to be ignorant of the deed for several years, the ghost of Pancho Villa knew, and began to haunt the hotel of this dishonorable man. His decapitated spirit still roams the hotel basement, searching for his head.

On a few excursions, we have been escorted by security to the basement catacombs. As we all prowled around in our sneakers, we heard the sounds of cowboy boots walking down the hall ahead of us.

Carmen, an elevator operator who has worked at the Gadsden for many years, has encountered Pancho's headless ghost twice. Both times, the ghost was wearing a black suit jacket with shiny shoes and had no head! Others have seen this specter wearing either a dress military uniform or a khaki uniform. I found old photographs of Pancho Villa wearing all three styles of dress.

Hotel manager Robin Brekhus had her own encounter with a ghost in the basement. The hotel's power had gone out in the middle of the afternoon, so she went down to the supply room with a flashlight to get candles for guests and staff. As Robin reached for the supply room door, she saw a shadowy ghost figure ahead of her. Was it Pancho? Robin didn't pause to find out. She grabbed the candles, turned around and ran!

The Gadsden Hotel was the host of our July 2001 Spirit Photography Workshop, an event attended by thirty-two ghost hunters. A lot of ghost activity and energy was detected throughout the night. Cold spots were felt and many ghost hunters photographed orbs. The psychics in attendance felt potent energies as soon as they entered the building.

Late at night, the hotel lights are dimmed with only the security lights in use. Clerks at the lobby desk have seen inexplicable shadows milling around the pillars or heard the sound of bare feet running across the tile floors. Many times security has also seen shadows moving about the mezzanine, almost as if a gala ball were about to begin.

Are you brave enough to spend a night where the shadows walk *alone*?

Address:	1046 G Avenue, Douglas, AZ 85607
Phone:	520-364-4481
Fax:	520-364-4005
Email:	robin@hotelgadsden.com
Website:	www.hotelgadsden.com
Contact:	Robin Brekhus, manager
Lodging:	130 rooms with private baths
Amenities:	TV, phone, dining room, tavern, salon, laundry

Ecto mists up close and personal in the Pirtleville Cemetery, Douglas, Arizona, during the Gadsden Hotel Spirit Photography Workshop.
(Photo by John Lamarca)

Comfi Cottages of Flagstaff
Flagstaff

History

Built in the early 20th century, these quaint cottages are scattered throughout various neighborhoods convenient to historic downtown Flagstaff. Each cottage was originally built as a residence, independent of the rest, and all were private residences until the 1980s when Pat and Ed Wiebe began to acquire and convert them into the hospitable vacation rentals they are today. They are all within easy walking distance of restaurants, shopping, parks, Northern Arizona University and Lowell Observatory.

The cottage to rent if you would like a paranormal roommate is located at 919 North Beaver Street. This three-bedroom cottage was built in 1937, and it belonged to the then-assistant postmaster whose eighteen-year-old daughter died from either whooping cough or kidney disease in the 1950s. As we sat in Pat's own cozy home, she showed us a picture (acquired after her neighbor's son married one of the girls in the photo and gave a copy to Pat) of a slumber party that had been held sometime during the 1950s in the living room, taken when the former owner's daughter and her friends were in their early teens.

A lady in her 60s who had attended this slumber party in her youth stopped by the cottage one day and had a strange deja vu experience, once again feeling the familiar presence of her long-dead friend.

The young woman passed on years before the other members of her family. Her father died in 1969, and her mother in 1992. When the home was purchased by Pat and Ed the son came into town to pick up a few personal belongings. He left behind several family photos and pictures of the cottage from his youth.

Ghosts

Team member Maddie, her daughter Megan and I drove to this cottage on a dreary, snowy day, but since none of us had seen snow in some time, it looked quite beautiful as it fell and covered the ground. When I hopped out of the truck to snap a picture, a large, black crow squawked and flew out from the branches of a nearby tree. What an appropriate omen to see so near the haunted cottage, I thought to myself.

A crow cawing and flying about (for those of you who are puzzled) often signifies death in some capacity. Traditionally revered as a messenger of the gods and the guardian who carries the soul to rebirth or the afterlife, there are many superstitions connected with crows (and ravens, who are in the same family). These birds are considered omens of both fortune and misfortune, depending on the culture and circumstances, and have been associated with death and the underworld, cross-culturally, from the earliest times. In folklore, crows are also associated with the sun, longevity, beginnings, change, spiritual strength and solitude. For example, in Brazil, there is a belief that the human soul can inhabit the body of a raven. Elsewhere, in old Europe, it was once believed that fairies turned into crows in order to cause mischief. An adage from Celtic folklore sums up the wide range of messages crows are thought to herald: "One crow—sorrow; two crows—mirth; three crows—wedding; four crows—birth." In this case, the crow I saw seemed to be a messenger of sorrow. The story we heard later about the ghost of the teenager who died there was enough to make the crow's appearance seem to foretell our coming sadness.

Various guests have encountered the young woman's ghost. Two elderly couples from the Midwest were staying in the cottage behind the larger cabin. After taking some laundry over to the other cottage, one of the ladies felt a presence upstairs. Startled but not frightened, she asked the Wiebes, "Is this place haunted?" Like all who have sensed the presence, she felt it was a peaceful spirit.

A psychic friend of Pat who stayed in the mini-cottage behind the house has also felt the presence of the ghost. Since the larger cottage was vacant, she had permission to use its laundry facilities. While she waited, she sat in the living room, reading a book and feeling fine, not expecting anything unusual. But when she moved into the kitchen, the spirit activity she encountered there caught her unawares and made her feel faint. As she stood there, collecting herself, she felt a spirit move past her and up the stairs.

Another guest reported an encounter with a female ghost who appeared to be in her late teens in the same upstairs bedroom. Perhaps this "teen angel" who died in the prime of her life does not realize that she has passed on. It seems that she still longs for slumber parties and human contact, so if you stay in the big cottage on Beaver Street, be prepared to make her acquaintance!

Address: 1612 North Aztec St., Flagstaff, AZ 86001
Phone: 928-774-0731; Toll Free: 888-774-0731
Fax: 928-773-7286
Email: pat@comficottages.com
Website: www.comficottages.com
Contact: Pat Wiebe, co-owner
Lodging: 7 fully-equipped vacation rental cottages
Amenities: breakfast foods in the fridge for guests to
              prepare, TV/VCR, telephone, down comforters,
              gas barbecue grill, picnic table, lawn furniture,
              bicycles, sleds, ice chests, picnic baskets

Hotel Monte Vista
Flagstaff

History

Hotel Monte Vista is one of the few American hotels built largely through public subscription. Tourism was on the rise in the booming economy of the 1920s, so the citizens of Flagstaff agreed that they needed to have a first-class hotel to keep out-of-towners in the area, pampered and contented, to spend their money and help the local economy thrive.

In 1924, astronomer V.M. Slipher headed up a local fund-raising effort which ultimately resulted in a city ordinance that established a municipal bond, held collectively by Flagstaff residents, to build the Hotel Monte Vista. Novelist Zane Grey put up the remainder of the money needed to build this impressive four-story structure of brick, steel and concrete. Constructed on a corner in the heart of town, the hotel was originally named the Flagstaff Community Hotel, and when it opened on New Year's Day, January 1, 1927, a contest was held to rename it. A twelve-year-old schoolgirl won with her submission *Monte Vista*, which means "mountain view" in Spanish. This new Hotel Monte Vista was billed as the first full-service hotel in Arizona and bragged of its running water, flushable toilets, telephones and room service, quite the modern amenities for its day.

Hotel Monte Vista is located one block away from famous Route 66. Many Hollywood stars whose movies were being filmed in and around the Flagstaff and Sedona areas have been guests here, so certain rooms are named after some of the most noteworthy celebrity guests. The list is impressive, including Humphrey Bogart, Bing Crosby, Debbie Reynolds, Michael J. Fox, Jane Russell, Gary Cooper, John Wayne, Spencer Tracy, Clark Gable, Carole Lombard, Bob Hope, Zane Grey and Esther Williams.

The hotel belonged to Flagstaff residents until the early 1960s when it was sold to a private individual. It was the longest publicly held commercial hotel in the history of America, and it continues to be the longest continuously running hotel in Flagstaff. Hotel Monte Vista's restoration process began in 1986, and since then, it has been returned to its original style and luster. Today, owned and operated by Jim Craven, it is on the National Register of Historic Places.

Ghosts

Team member Maddie, her daughter Megan and I arrived at the Hotel Monte Vista on a Sunday afternoon. Kelly Greenwalt, a (former) front desk clerk, was on hand to greet us. She was very interested in the Monte Vista ghosts and had been keeping a notebook filled with newspaper articles on the hotel and stories of its haunts. After deciding to start our ghost tour at the top, we headed for the fourth floor where we could begin to review the hotel's ghost stories.

Although the fourth floor is usually not as active as the others, it has been the backdrop to a goodly share of ghost stories. Room 402 is the John Wayne Suite, where John Wayne stayed when he was filming westerns in the area. The Duke himself reported having a ghostly experience in this room. One version of the story (there are quite a few) has it that in the late 1950s, he walked into the sitting room area of his suite and encountered a friendly spirit standing near a table. The story doesn't tell us if the ghost was a cowboy or not.

Down on the third floor, ghost hunter Megan Taylor had a profound ghost encounter. While she and her husband were guests at the Monte Vista for an anniversary weekend, they decided to stay in the John Wayne Suite. Not detecting anything out of the ordinary in their room, Megan grabbed her digital camera and set out to explore. Descending the stairs and starting down the halls of the third floor, she spotted an orb in front of her and began to follow it down the hall. Looking up, she saw what appeared to be a man at his door, going through the motions of unlocking it with his key. Megan said the spirit looked as real as you or me. But instead of opening the door, he walked right through it. Incidentally, this ghost bore a striking resemblance to actor Alan Ladd and was entering Room 309–the Alan Ladd Room.

It is rumored that in the 1940s two prostitutes were murdered and their bodies were thrown out of a third floor window. Since then, numerous guests staying on the third floor have reported the feeling of being watched. Perhaps the ladies' ghosts roam the halls; their presence is often felt in Room 306, the likely but undocumented crime scene.

Room 305, nicknamed the Rocking Chair Room, gained some public renown when it was featured on an episode of *Unsolved Mysteries*. Each time a guest entered the room, the rocking chair had a reputation for being in a different spot. Most of the time, regardless of wherever it wound up, the chair would be facing toward the window, almost as if some-one was watching for the return of a loved one. A rocking chair is still in the room, and guests are still finding it situated the same way near the window. Some guests have even reported seeing a female spirit sitting in the chair at night.

While I was filming the walk-through segment of our tour in Room 305, the sound of a rocking chair creaking back and forth was recorded on tape. When I played the videotape back, I could hear the distinct creak of what sounded like a chair in motion. Just to check that it wasn't squeaky door hinges creaking, I called the hotel and asked them to move the room's door back and forth. The hinges did not make a sound.

The second floor is also quite an active place for ghosts. In Room 210, the Zane Grey Suite (also known as the Phantom Bellboy Room), guests have reported hearing a phantom bellboy who knocks at the door, announcing, "Room service!" in a muffled voice. When they have opened the door, guests have not found anyone there nor have they seen anyone running away down the long corridor.

Apparently, some ghosts like to make prank calls. If you stay in Room 216–the room of the mysterious phone calls–be prepared for some rude awakenings. The phone often rings in the middle of the night, but when it is answered, there is no one on the line. All that can be heard is "dead air."

One of the last rooms in the hotel to be rented out is typically Room 220, the last room on the left at the end of the second floor hallway. This particular room seems to have an eerie ghost vibration that most people find spooky. There is an overwhelming feeling of sadness that pervades it and seems to be connected with one of the room's former guests. In the early 1980s, a strange, long-term boarder called this room home. He spent long periods of time isolated here and was known to indulge in a wide range of eccentric behaviors that included hanging raw meat from the chandelier (as a result, his ghost has the dubious honor of being tagged with our nickname, "The Meatman"). After he passed away in the room, because of his hermit-like habits, the man went unmissed, and his body lay decomposing for two or three days. And now, it seems that the man's ghost refuses to check out of his onetime Monte Vista residence.

An example of the room's bizarre ghost currents: A maintenance man who had been doing repairs in the room turned off the light, locked the door and left. He returned five minutes later to find the light back on, the bedding stripped and the TV blaring full blast. A former bar manager saw a ghost while she was temporarily residing in Room 222. After returning from a night of bartending, the woman lay down to rest and happened to look to her right where she saw an old man in his 70s with gray hair, wearing a white shirt. He vanished after she spied him there. Sleep was a little long in coming to her that night.

On the lowest level, the cocktail room has its tales, too. In 1970, three men robbed the bank next door, and before the heist, the gunmen made a vow to have a drink together in the hotel bar after they had completed their "mission." But during their attempted getaway, one of the robbers was shot and fatally wounded by a security guard. Remembering their promise, however, the dying man dragged himself into the bar to have one last drink with his partners before he expired on the premises.

Now it seems that the bank robber's ghost haunts the lounge. Bartenders and patrons alike have reported strange things, like bar stools sliding across the floor on their own, disembodied voices greeting the owner and the TV channels changing without anyone using the remote.

The last segment of our tour brought us into the Monte Vista's basement. Whatever happened down there years ago is unknown, but night auditors sometimes hear a baby's crying coming through the basement door late at night.

The Hotel Monte Vista welcomes ghost hunters and will be happy to book you a room, perhaps with the ghost of one of your favorite stars from yesteryear. Or maybe you will be one of the few to brave the peculiar melancholy of Room 220. Whatever you do, if you visit, be prepared for the unusual!

Address:	100 North San Francisco Street, Flagstaff, AZ 86001
Phone:	928-779-6971; Toll Free: 800-545-3068
Fax:	928-779-2904
Email:	montev@infomagic.net
Website:	www.hotelmontevista.com
Contact:	Jim Craven, owner
Lodging:	50 rooms and suites
Amenities:	gift shop, hair salon, lounge, phone, cable TV, laundry room

Weatherford Hotel
Flagstaff

History

John W. Weatherford (1859-1934), a native of Weatherford, Texas, built the Weatherford Hotel in 1898. The hotel was originally a smaller building containing a general store on the first floor, along with a residence for the Weatherford family upstairs. Weatherford's vision of a grander, more genteel establishment was realized on New Year's Day 1900, when the Weatherfords celebrated the grand opening of a three-story hotel addition. The improvements in the expanded hotel must have awed the visitors that day in the pioneer town, both local mountaineers and out-of-towners alike.

Some of the hotel's outstanding new features included a new ballroom, surrounded by a three-sided balcony. The bar within the ballroom featured an elaborately carved counter from the Palace Hotel Saloon in Tombstone, with stunningly wrought, inlaid stained glass ornamentation. Also on the top floor was the sunroom (eventually converted into more guest rooms). While this upper level was ideal for celebrations like parties and dances, the bottom floor lent itself to more practical uses, such as providing a place for civic groups to meet. Although a fire damaged the balcony and original cupola in 1929, recent reconstruction and renovation efforts have reanimated the magnificence of the hotel's past.

For many years, this was *the* place to be in town. The Weatherford was regarded by many as Flagstaff's most distinguished hotel, so much so that famous guests like publisher William Randolph Hearst, artist Thomas Moran and writer Zane Grey stayed here. Grey even penned one of his novels, *The Call of the Canyon*, within the ballroom later to be named after him.

The Weatherford has worn some different hats through the years, at points housing a theater, billiard hall and radio station as well as several restaurants since it opened over a century ago, all while continuing to function as a hotel. After purchasing it in 1975 (and rescuing the old structure from the wrecking ball), Henry Taylor and Sam Green-Taylor's ongoing historical preservation efforts have won them several awards, particularly for their work on the balcony and ballroom. In the same vein, they have opted for decor that maintains the turn-of-the-century look running throughout the hotel. There are three bars to choose from, all of which offer unique atmospheres, and one restaurant adjacent to the hotel called Charly's Pub & Grill (which contains one of the watering holes), based in a small brick building that housed Flagstaff's first phone company, the Telephone Exchange. This restaurant was also built by Weatherford and has been restored to its original 1909 character.

Today's Weatherford Hotel is a peaceful, hospitable place to relax, soak up some history—perhaps meet a ghost or two.

Ghosts

Dave Campbell, an employee of the Weatherford, seemed very enthused about sharing the hotel's ghost stories as he graciously escorted team member Maddie Herrick, her daughter Megan and me around the building. Proudly handing me a flyer about the history of the hotel, he escorted us up to the recently renovated Zane Grey Ballroom on the third floor and into the bar area. Dave directed our attention to the object of several ghost reports, the beautiful old bar from Tombstone. People have seen drinks sliding down the length of it (and probably wondered if they'd had a few too many when it happened). It is possible that some of Tombstone's energies became attached to the bar, imprinting upon it to create such phenomena after it was transplanted.

There has been at least one report of a ballroom ghost. A couple happened to be in the ballroom early one morning, around 5:30 a.m., when they saw the ghostly figure of a girl floating across the room.

Next, Dave led us to a hallway on the third floor where he often hears his name being called out by some unseen spirit. He is not alone in this experience; other co-workers have experienced the same sensation. When it happens, he said that it feels as if someone is standing behind him, looking over his shoulder.

Flicking on the light in Room 54, Dave related a disturbing story about a couple who rented the room long ago. The couple began to quarrel, and their arguing became so intense that a murder took place! Many times guests have reported seeing a man and woman enter Room 54, which would not be unusual except for one thing: today Room 54 is only a storage closet.

Inside Room 54, Dave guided us over to the former bathroom (now a moproom/washroom). He told me that another ghost hunter was able to photograph orbs in here on her night vision camcorder.

A former employee of the Weatherford had an alarming experience while staying in one of the upstairs rooms. She awoke in the middle of the night to find a couple sitting on her bed, looking as real as you or me, until they got up and walked *through* the door.

For the last leg of our tour, Dave slipped us through the kitchen into a back stairway that led to the basement, sharing the traumatic story of Noah. Noah was a bootlegger during the Prohibition era who sold his whiskey in these dark, cluttered, unrefined catacombs. Legend has it that he was murdered and robbed down here by another bootlegger. Although I did not sense an evil presence at all, most of the staff is afraid to venture down here. (I detected feelings of entrapment, loneliness and sadness.)

Noah's body was removed, but his ghost remains. Sam's late dog, Mona, had problems with the basement, often refusing to cross a certain area no matter how much she was coaxed. Kitchen workers often hear Noah's ghost walking up and down the basement steps. None of the staff willingly sets foot in the basement for it is said that Noah still prowls in the gloom of the basement where he ran his illegal business, in search of his killer.

If you're game for a shot or two of adrenaline, some goose bumps and a really wily invisible bartender, come to the Weatherford Hotel. Experience its history for yourself, and discover what spine-tingling really means!

Address:	23 North Leroux, Flagstaff, AZ 86001
Phone:	928-779-1919
Fax:	928-773-8951
Email:	contact@weatherfordhotcl.com
Website:	www.weatherfordhotel.com
Contact:	Henry Taylor and Sam Green-Taylor, owners
Lodging:	8 rooms: 5 with private baths and 3 with shared
Amenities:	most rooms have 1 double bed with no TV or phone, restaurants and bars below, ballroom

Noftsger Hill Inn
Globe

History

The Noftsger Hill Inn sits high on a hill overlooking the city of Globe and dates back to 1907, when it was known as the North Globe Schoolhouse. As miners flocked to work in Globe's copper mines, a larger school became necessary to serve the needs of the community; this much larger building was established to fill that need . In 1917, the front half of the existing structure was added, and the name changed to the Noftsger Hill School, after Globe businessman A. N. Noftsger (the hill it sits upon bore his name first). Noftsger made his living by supplying local miners and their families with a resource more precious than Globe's silver or copper: water (he had purchased the area's water rights). The school that bore Noftsger's name educated many generations of children until 1981, when the schoolhouse closed its doors for more than just the summer. Here, school was finally out for good.

A renovation process began ten years later to change this landmark school into the bright, spacious and charming Inn it is today. Rooms at the front of the building provide views of the Pinal Mountains and the city of Globe. The rooms in the back look out onto the historic Old Dominion Mine.

(Sidenote: One of Noftsger Hill School's most famous students is former Arizona Governor Rose Mofford.)

Ghosts

Ghost hunter Megan Taylor and I met Rosalie Ayala, one of the owners/innkeepers, on a Saturday afternoon. She greeted us at the doors of the old schoolhouse and brought us into a large common area filled with antiques. As we went deeper into the building, we walked through a hallway lined with class pictures from school days long past.

Rosalie related that she had never seen anything to convince her that the Inn was haunted but shared that the neighborhood children apparently have a different opinion. They are convinced that the ghost of a mean schoolteacher still walks the halls, haunting the Inn. The youngsters have even told Rosalie that the bones of the teacher are buried in the basement. (Of course, this is just urban legend; there is no evidence to support such a claim.) She said the children are so afraid of this "ghost" that they refuse to come to the Inn's front door to trick-or-treat on Halloween; Rosalie accommodates their fears by going down to the stairs near the sidewalk to hand out candy.

Many former students come back to the Inn (as well as former students who are no longer alive!). They talk, wander about and reminisce about the "evil" (or, more likely, the strictest) teacher who instructed them in their youth.

I spoke to a former Globe resident who remembered roller-skating on the school grounds when the building was vacant. She told me that lights would sometimes turn on and off in various classrooms, and she and her friends would often hear a telephone ringing inside.

Rosalie escorted us upstairs to investigate some of the rooms. The staircase on the right side of the building provided us with considerable paranormal activity. Megan's EMF meter began to record high readings, and I began to photograph large orbs in that same location. Rosalie, although skeptical, was interested in what our digital cameras were recording when we went downstairs into the expansive dining area. Once again, large orbs showed up when we viewed the shots later on computer.

Recently, on a second trip, Megan and I returned to the Inn as overnight guests. After being assigned to Room 2, we unpacked our ghost-hunting equipment and placed a few toys and marbles on the floor in hopes that child spirits would want to play with them. We settled in to watch for movement.

As Megan and I sat in rocking chairs in the middle of the room, we began to plan our strategy for the evening. After about fifteen to twenty minutes had passed, Megan glanced at the leather reading chair and spotted an apparition of an elderly, partially bald, white-haired gentleman with long sideburns. He leaned forward as if he were interested in our conversation, and then, without warning, he disappeared.

When the next ghost appeared, Megan saw small feet (from the ankles down) running across the floor, past the chalkboard. She looked again and saw what appeared to be a small, barefoot boy. He was wearing overalls and had disheveled hair. I was able to discern the filmy outline of a small, child-sized shadow. The vivid image I received in my mind's eye coupled with my sixth sense led me to believe we had encountered a tomboy, not a real "boy." I also noted the child was wearing overalls, but to me, she appeared to be a girl, with short, sandy blonde hair in a blunt, bowl-style cut with bangs. We both felt that the child was from the 1920s or early 1930s.

Venturing into the hallway, we perused the many class photos displayed on the walls, hoping to identify the ghosts we had seen in our room. To our delight, we found a picture of the gentleman spirit we had seen earlier in the chair! We also located the photo of a small barefoot boy wearing denims, in addition to several photos of little girls with that same blunt haircut. Rosalie confirmed that Room 2 was the old kindergarten and first grade classroom, which was corroborated by the size of the "child" we had seen.

Later on, I was standing near the foot of Megan's bed, talking about our discovery, when a very strange thing happened. Something emerged from underneath the bed and bumped up against the outside of my right foot. I felt a slight punch, jumped and looked down to see a dark shadowy ball retracting backward, out of sight. I had been standing too far away from the bed to have accidentally bumped into the frame. Although I immediately got down on my hands and knees to inspect under the bed, nothing was there. It had completely vanished!

Rosalie said that past guests have asked her if the Inn is haunted, but she had always responded that she didn't think so, despite the following eerie predawn incident. Rosalie admitted that she heard footsteps on the hardwood floors when her husband was away on business and she was the only person in the building. Thinking he had returned early, she got up and turned on the lights, only to find herself alone. Watching us on the trail of ghosts seemed to be enough to make her reconsider her experience.

After observing our investigation, Rosalie said she could now tell guests it is very possible that there may be lingering spirits present. Perhaps the ghosts of dedicated schoolteachers, or mischievous students who had to stay after class to clean erasers abide within the Noftsger Hill Inn.

Address:	425 North Street, Globe, AZ 85501
Phone:	928-425-2260; Toll free: 877-780-2479
Fax:	928-402-8235
Email:	info@noftsgerhillinn.com
Website:	www.noftsgerhillinn.com
Contact:	Rosalie and Dom Ayala, owners
Lodging:	6 guest rooms
Amenities:	spacious guest rooms, each with a sitting area, fireplace, original chalkboards "decorated" with comments from past guests, private bathroom

Connor Hotel
Jerome

History

David Connor, an Irish immigrant, built the Connor Hotel in Jerome during 1898, presumably because the great copper mining boom of the late 1800s had created a considerable demand for places to put up the area's business travelers. Stones for the structure were quarried from the nearby hills. The Connor Hotel was a victim of Jerome's fire-prone conditions, and it burned down twice, along with the rest of the town, before the turn of the century. The third rebuilding effort proved to be the charm. Business flourished.

Connor had first erected a one-story stone building called the Stone Saloon on this site. As the town grew and business boomed, he invested his fortunes into the business and expanded it into a hotel. This hotel became an establishment with twenty-six rooms upstairs—all quite small—rented on the European plan (for which guests were charged full room plus board, rather than just room fees) for a mere $1.00 per night (mere by modern-day standards, anyway). Baths were located down the hall. Each room had a wood stove for heat and call bell for service. It was on the cutting edge of technology for the region, enjoying the status of being one of the first buildings in Jerome to be fully electric.

The Connor Hotel offered its guests a saloon complete with card rooms and billiard tables on the first floor. The local ladies of the night were not able to use the upstairs for their profession because the rooms were too expensive. At the west end of the building, however, was a false storefront that led to an alleyway known as Husband's Alley, which led to the scarlet women.

1931 marked the year the hotel began its decline. The parents of Anne Conlin, the current manager of the hotel, bought the hotel in 1980 and continued to rent out rooms for a rather insubstantial fee up until the late 1980s, when they shut down until renovations could be made to the old building. In 1999, the Conlin family began restoring the Connor Hotel, ultimately reopening for business on October 6, 2000. The number of rooms reduced from twenty to ten, with the rooms doubling in size and finally containing private bathrooms. The contractor, Harry Stewart, took great pains to preserve and restore all of the unique, original interior features, such as doors, windows, trimwork and transoms, even saving two walls of the original wallpaper in Room 3, as well as smaller patches of wallpaper in other areas. It now has updated wiring and plumbing along with all the modern conveniences and comforts desired for a weekend getaway. It also has a colorful past wrapped in stories that seem to keep spirits checking into their favorite rooms periodically.

Ghosts

Ghost hunter Megan Taylor and I were eager to meet Anne Conlin, manager of the Connor Hotel. She took us back to her office where we sat down to hear tales of the ghosts that walk the halls of the old building. It turns out that her very first guest had an extremely distressing ghostly experience.

It was about a week before the grand opening of the new Connor Hotel, and a man from Phoenix was installing a new satellite dish system. Everything was in place, except for a few minor things which would have to wait until the following day. Anne asked the installer if he would have the honor of being her first guest and thereby avoid driving down to Cottonwood to get a room. He accepted her invitation, and she picked out the prettiest room in the hotel—Room 1—a spacious, gorgeous corner room that sits over the bar with windows in two directions. Anne knew of the room's haunted history and reputation, but she did not want to alarm her first guests and so said nothing about it. She put the new towels in the room, fluffed up the pillows and proudly escorted her honored guest to his room.

The following morning when everyone showed up for work, she asked the installer, "How did it go? How was your night?" He was very quiet for a moment. She probed a little more. "Fine, fine," is all he would mutter in response. Anne let the questions drop.

Later that day, as she was giving a room tour to the bar manager, she mentioned the hotel's ghostly history. The installer, working nearby, happened to overhear her.

"I didn't want to say anything," he said, "but I was frightened last night and slept in my van." Anne sat down with him as he related his story: During the night, a lady's whispering had woken him up. He tried to block it from his mind. He couldn't. He tried to endure it by turning up the radio. It continued. Suddenly, an icy chill traveled up his body until it had engulfed him completely. He was terrified. Not stopping for his belongings, not pausing to lock the door behind him, he fled out of the building to his van; he spent the rest of the night there.

When the other construction workers at the hotel got wind of this story, they had a big laugh at his expense and teased him mercilessly. (Whether any of *them* could have fared any better under such circumstances, however, is open to debate.) Since then, guests in Room 1 have repeatedly had similar experiences, even feeling that same coldness.

One of the desk clerks has a golden retriever she brings to work, and the dog is very people-friendly. One day she had to run upstairs to deliver some towels to a guest in Room 2. Her dog followed her up the steps, which was not unusual, and she left him in the room's doorway as she ran down to the linen room to grab the towels, thinking he would lie down. Instead, the golden retriever responded bizarrely to the room, whining and causing a racket. He would not go into the room without her. The normally well-adjusted dog's behavior and refusal to enter the room alone made the hairs on the back of her neck stand straight up. Whatever he was able to sense in the room was invisible to her.

On a different day, an incident in Room 2 became a housekeeping issue. The same front desk clerk–being very particular about how the rooms appear when they are pre- pared for guests–had pushed the desk chair snugly up to the desk. When she returned a little later, the chair had moved so that it was sitting at the window. No one else had entered the room while she was gone.

Room 5 is a smaller, charming room—a smaller, charm- ing room where electrical appliances continually go haywire. Electricians have checked the system many times but to no avail; there is no bad wiring (bear in mind that it had all been replaced during renovation). The problem is not only with things that plug into the walls, either. Guests' cell phones, palm pilots and laptop computers malfunction here, too. The alarm on the room's clock radio goes off now and again, sometimes days after guests have departed. And the satellite TV has had more problems in here than in any other room. It somehow zaps itself.

A guest came down to the front desk one morning and complained that the dog in Room 5 would not stop growling. She stated that she heard it growling from under the door when she passed by. There was only one problem with her complaint: there *was* no dog in the room. For that matter, there was no human in the room. The room was empty.

One of the housekeepers had an experience that validated the room's growling dog phenomenon. This woman admitted she was afraid to go in Room 5 because she periodically heard a dog growling. Her first reaction was that a guest had left his pet behind. But as time passed and the growling continued without an actual dog ever turning up, she became spooked and began to avoid the room altogether.

Guests have reported hearing what sounds like a man coughing in this same room.

Could one of these orbs be Room 9's ghost in the bowler hat?

(Photo by Lisa McDaniel)

Room 9 is not a room the Conlins get many haunted reports on (although one of the housekeepers who is quite sensitive feels a presence here), so the next story is doubly remarkable because it happened when a very sensible couple was staying here. When one of these very rational guests came down to the front desk after the episode concluded, she related this story to the clerk: She had been coming out of the bathroom when she beheld a very strange sight–what she described as a small man standing behind her husband, wearing a bowler hat and a dark suit. She tried to make out his face but could not as it was blurry, like she was looking at it through someone else's glasses. When she told her husband to turn around and look, the man was gone.

After telling us these stories, Anne took Megan and me upstairs to show us these haunted rooms. As we began our tour, Megan photographed an orb on the stair landing. We could not help but notice that the pictures on the walls had to be straightened every time we passed by them.

Our dowsing rods popped apart as we approached Room 5, and the EMF meters were in the caution zone. All this activity is likely due to a high energy field present within the room. Although our dowsing rods popped apart as we neared the door, once inside we found that the energy field was contained inside the room's walls. We also discovered that the door shuts behind you. This is possibly due to the fact that the room tilts slightly from the settling of the building, so that gravity is the actual invisible force closing it, but it does contribute to the room's eerie feel!

Out of the blue, a brilliant idea occurred to me, and I asked

The MVD Ghostchasers pose with the Connor
Hotel Spirit Photography Workshop participants.

Anne if the MVD Ghostchasers could conduct the July 2002 Spirit Photography Workshop in the Connor Hotel. She was very excited and agreed to let us rent the entire hotel for a Saturday night. Amazingly, we booked every room and had twenty-four people participate in the workshop, with eight MVD Ghostchasers and sixteen guests present. The event, which lasted from Saturday afternoon through Sunday morning, produced quite a few discoveries.

Two psychics immediately felt the presence of a young girl in the lobby, standing near Anne's office. Later, another psychic arrived and confirmed the same revelation. At this point, the girl was still in the lobby but standing near a glass counter. This second psychic felt that the girl had bled to

You never know if you're hunting the ghosts or if the ghosts are hunting you!
(Photo by Lisa McDaniel)

death outside the Connor's front door.

The same psychic witnessed the spirit of a man climbing up the stairs. She saw him stop and rest his hand on the rail as if another man had come down the steps to talk to him.

During her stay, this psychic shared Room 3 with her daughter, and she saw the spirit of a man standing in the bathroom doorway. She could tell that he was slightly built and standing with his hands in his pockets. She was also able to make out that his hair and beard were gray.

We spent the night exploring the hotel and areas nearby the Connor. After we ate dinner at the Haunted Hamburger (haunted as the name suggests), we toured the Jerome Cemetery and took a haunted ghost-walking tour with a town historian. Our guest psychics performed regressions for part of the team while others took advantage of this quiet time to take pictures of orbs on the stairway and in the halls and rooms. Until about 3:00 a.m., we hunted for ghosts. At about 3:30 a.m., B.J. Woolley and I lay down on the floor and filmed orbs floating by in the ceiling skylights.

Although no apparitions were caught on film, it was a night enjoyed by all. And even though I left dog biscuits inside and outside of Room 5, ghost hunter Mark Christoph reported that no growling dog appeared in his room during the night.

Address:	164 Main Street, P.O. Box 1177, Jerome, AZ 86331
Phone:	928-634-5006; Toll Free: 800-523-3554
Fax:	928-649-0981
Email:	connor@sedona.net
Website:	www.connorhotel.com
Contact:	Anne Conlin, manager
Lodging:	10 rooms with private, tiled baths
Amenities:	satellite TV, VCR, phone, hair dryer, coffee maker, microwave, mini refrigerator, bar, king and queen beds, pets allowed (but only if they promise not to growl in Room 5!)

Ghost City Inn
Bed & Breakfast
Jerome

History

The Ghost City Inn is one of the first Bed and Breakfasts you see as you wind your way up Cleopatra Hill into the town of Jerome, designated a National Historic District in 1967. You can sit on the Inn's veranda, sip your tea and watch the traffic come and go in this peaceful little community perched on the mountain.

The Inn was originally built around 1890 as a boarding house for employees of the nearby copper mines. One of the few wooden structures untouched by Jerome's string of fires, it was sturdily constructed with some intended clientele in mind–middle mining management–having nine foot ceilings and large rooms. Later, it was known as the Garcia house, after the family who owned it as a private residence for almost forty years, from 1920 till 1959. Its brief stint as a bootleg liquor factory lasted until the still blew up, damaging the upper floor in the process (some evidence from this explosion is still visible). Sometime in the late 60s, it operated briefly as an ashram, and then the building was purchased by a lady who turned it into a restaurant called Maude's. After that, it became a duplex until its latest transformation; in 1994, it was purchased by a group of investors who handled the conversion and refurbishing of the building into a Bed and Breakfast. Each guest room was uniquely decorated according to a theme that connects to local culture, past and present.

Ghost City Inn is named as such because "Ghost City" is the town's nickname; after the mines closed in the 50s, Jerome became one of the largest ghost towns in the nation. Although it was revived to a thriving artistic community, Jerome is a place where the haunts of bygone days still dwell. The hosts of the Inn say it may be haunted, but they prefer to leave that determination up to their guests.

Ghosts

Several ghost sightings have been reported here. The vicinities of the Cleopatra Hill Room and the Verde View Room tend to generate the most ghost reports. But throughout the building, people witness doors slamming shut by themselves and hear voices when nobody else is present.

I traveled with team members Kenton Moore and Chris and Shiela McCurdy to investigate the Ghost City Inn on one of the first Sundays of spring. It seems we came at a good time because there had been a lot of recent paranormal activity all through the building. Innkeeper Jackie Muma met us at the door and focused our attention on the Cleopatra Hill Room, where there have been quite a few sightings of a female spirit.

A little background: Grandma Garcia resided in the Cleopatra Hill Room when she owned the boarding house, and she reputedly hated smoking. Many times guests have found that their lighters and cigarettes have been hidden or moved from where they were placed. Does she still reside here?

Grandma Garcia's tiny 4' 9" transparent form has been seen moving within her former room. Her granddaughter confirmed she could feel her presence when she stayed in the room. Guests have reported that personal items placed on the table often seem misplaced but then show up later, either back on the table or in a purse. They typically feel that she is a protective spirit (maybe a trifle ornery), and it is not uncommon for guests to feel as if they have been "tucked in" by her at night. It may be that she still lingers here so she can gaze out to the beauty of the Verde Valley almost a mile below.

We pulled out our digital cameras, EMF meters and thermal scanners to look for variations in the room. There were no major readings on the devices, but we did photograph a faint orb in the bathroom area.

Upstairs in the Northern Exposure Room, Jackie told us about a ghost report she had received just the day before from a guest who had spent the night here: The woman felt a spirit touching her face in the hours before dawn. It also tried to pull down her covers. She and her partner didn't sleep much the rest of the night.

In the upstairs hall outside the Verde View Room, there have been reports of a very real-looking male spirit who takes on solid form, repeatedly described as a gray figure, dressed in a long duster. This older-looking cowboy has long gray hair but no hat, and he usually looks like he just came off a long trail ride. The room's veranda looks out onto a cemetery on the side of a hill about one-half-mile away from which some of the Inn's spirits may have strayed, including this one. Perhaps the ghosts of miners and cowboys buried in the nearby graveyard are not yet ready to leave their old boarding house?

Jackie had her own encounter with the cowboy one afternoon at about 2:30 p.m. She was upstairs vacuuming the common area, preparing for her next group of guests, when she saw the dusty cowboy walk into the hall bathroom. Thinking that a man had just wandered in off the street, she went after the cowboy to inform him that their restroom facilities were not open to the public. But as he entered the bathroom, the man disappeared. Jackie thought he might be hiding and boldly opened the shower stall to find it was empty. The dusty cowboy had vanished!

Guests have noted that this ghost appears around 2:30,

both in the a.m. *and* p.m. Such consistent timing might indicate what his former schedule was; perhaps this was the time of shift change when the mines ran 24/7.

Some guests have tried to contact the cowboy on a spirit board. He (assuming they successfully contacted their target) gave them the name J. Stark. Surprisingly, a man by the same name lived in Jerome many years ago, although we cannot determine if this is his spirit.

We found the Verde View Room the most interesting and perhaps the most active room in the Inn. While investigating it, the MVD Ghostchasers invited J. Stark to join us and appear before our cameras. EMF meters rose to 1.5, indicating slight spirit activity, and Shiela felt a heavy energy near the inside entryway. I immediately snapped a photo of a nice-sized orb up against the empty wall and assumed it was our cowboy trying to come through to us. Needless to say, we want to go back and spend the night when we can see for ourselves if J. Stark prepares himself for the 2:30 night shift!

Address:	541 Main Street, P.O. Box T, Jerome, AZ 86331
Phone:	928-63-GHOST (928-634-4678)
	Toll Free: 888-63-GHOST (888-634-4778)
Fax:	928-634-4678
Email:	reservations@ghostcityinn.com
Website:	www.ghostcityinn.com
Contact:	Allen and Jackie Muma, owners
Lodging:	6 uniquely stylized rooms
Amenities:	full breakfast served, cozy fireplace, TV, VCR, ceiling fans, hot tub, upper and lower verandas

The Inn at Jerome

Jerome

History

J. H. Clinkscalc, an insurance adjuster from Los Angeles, built the two-story structure that houses the Inn at Jerome after another fire raged through the town in 1899; this was the third time the town built of wood had been consumed by flames in two years. Clinksdale wanted his new building to be fireproof, so he had it constructed using reinforced concrete, with walls eighteen inches thick. Thanks to its sturdy construction, the building didn't burn down, and it never faltered during the endless dynamite blasting in the mines that caused businesses across the street to slide down the hill!

Originally, the building was a hardware store on the lower level with offices upstairs. It has fostered several other businesses as well: a mortuary, bordello and now, an inn. Once known as "The Wickedest Town in the West," during its prime, Jerome was anything but the peaceful, artistic community it is today. It was a wild and violent mining town—even more so than Tombstone—where the ruthless code of the Old West was in effect. The building's history appropriately contains pieces of that sordid past.

Owners Mark and Carla Butler purchased the building in

1994, updating and renovating the Inn to its current character. Reminiscent of Jerome's rustic turn-of-the-century look,
the Inn at Jerome offers guests a cozy and relaxed atmosphere
where the past is conjured and experienced. Ghosts from
bygone days stir in these walls, too, hinting at the secrets and
memories buried here.

Ghosts

Ghost hunter Megan Taylor and I interviewed Juanita
Schuyler in her office near the entrance to the rooms of the
Inn. She related a number of ghost tales to us that she and her
husband, Dennis, have experienced through the years, as well
as those reported by guests and employees. Nearly every
room of the Inn at Jerome has a story.

Spooky yet harmless paranormal activity has become
almost commonplace at the Inn. Consider, for a moment, the
bizarre events in a room called the Victorian Rose. One day,
after polishing the furniture with lemon oil, Juanita was on
her way out of the room when a vase that had been on the
dresser careened through the air, over her shoulder, crashing
to pieces on the hallway floor in front of her. Juanita replaced
the vase and relocated it to a different spot, on an antique
table that was in front of a window.

About a year after the vase incident, a housekeeper
entered the room and saw the replacement vase take off over
the bed, landing in front of the dresser. As if this repeated
phenomenon was not strange enough, this time, the vase did
not break. You can see this resilient "ghost missile" for
yourself, standing on top of the same dresser on a lace runner.

Also in the Victorian Rose Room, a different housekeeper
witnessed the shadow of a man moving across the room until
he disappeared behind a closet door. It appeared that the
shadow slid "behind" it, so she checked inside the closet but
found no evidence of ghosts or anything else unusual there.

Many guests have reported smelling perfume and the
distinct odor of hair-perming solution while staying in this
room. The smells arrive together, as if a female spirit is
applying a home permanent to her hair or has just had her

hair permed. But as quickly as the odor arrives, it just as quickly disappears. (Who from the Inn's past might be wearing strong perfume and getting her hair permed?)

One night, in the Memories of the Heart Room, guests were preparing to turn in for the evening. After locking and bolting the door, they soon fell fast asleep. The couple woke up later as the door cracked open, permitting a beam of light to illuminate the room. Astonished, they watched as, moments later, the door quietly closed itself. They arose from bed to check the door, and discovered it was still locked and bolted, as they had left it. Since the sound of a deadbolt locking is very noticeable, they would have heard it sliding back into place after it closed had it slid out of place in the first place while they were sleeping.

And that's not all that happens in the Memories of the Heart Room. Recently, a couple who spent the night in this room reported an experience they had that went beyond eerie. Evidently, there was a lot of supernatural activity occurring in the room during the night, and they had huddled together underneath the covers, more than a little spooked. At some point during the long night, a cold wind blew through the room, whipping underneath the covers and blowing the blankets and quilt completely off the bed.

There is an impish spirit in the Lariat and Lace Room who demands that housekeepers clean this room before the others. (There is less prankster activity in the room if they do; thus housekeeping complies with the implicit "request." An example of the mischief that this ghost wreaks follows). Once, as a housekeeper was leaving the room, a water glass flew off the table and hit her in the back. When Juanita went up later to investigate, she found no trace of any glasses until she heard glasses rattle and looked up to see them on top of a large armoire. Even if somebody had been in the room with her (they hadn't), you cannot reach the top of the armoire without a ladder!

In this same room, another housekeeper reported feeling someone watch her as she worked. Then she saw shadows moving away until they finally disappeared.

Housekeepers report that, after preparing the Pillow Talk Room and the Kiss and Tell Room for guests, they can return minutes later to see the impression of a person's body and head on the comforter and pillow. Moreover, the doors to the armoire in the Kiss and Tell Room are known to open of their own accord. Wall hangings are either rearranged or tucked away inside this haunted armoire.

Juanita spied a ghost inside the Pillow Talk Room as she was walking down the hall one day. She noted that he was leaning against the window frame, looking down into the alley; his unique appearance made an impression on her: work pants tucked into the top of his mid-calf work boots, with an old felt hat on top of his head, suspenders and a long-sleeved work shirt. She wasn't able to make out what colors he was wearing because he was hazy, cloaked in tones of grey. What she had seen did not fully register until she was past the room. Thinking that perhaps her imagination was playing tricks on her, she went back to confirm what she had just seen. Nothing was there, although a moment before, she vividly recalls that this man had been standing at the window.

Ghost hunters who have investigated the Spooks, Ghosts and Goblins Room have reported equipment malfunctions during their visits.

One particular ghost-hunting team took several photographs in this room. One photo revealed a ghost team member as she stood in front of a large mirror, with what appeared to be a transparent ghost cat overlaying her hair, occupying the same space where her head was, two-dimensionally. I noted that it seemed as if the cat was curled up in her hair. Was this documentation just another equipment malfunction? Or is it likely that this is one of the ghost "house" cats reported to inhabit the Inn?

There is some evidence to support the ghost cat theory: that this photo captured one of the resident ghost cats. These animal ghosts leave foot imprints and curled-up indentations on the bedspreads. Numerous guests have reported feeling something invisible rubbing up against their legs while they are in the restaurant. And something invisible and low-to-the-ground has been reported chasing mint candies from room to room, passing them paw to paw down the hall and hitting them with one swift swat so that they fly neatly down to the end of the hallway.

Dennis and Juanita have both heard someone making a "Pssst!" noise (the sound a person makes when trying to get your attention) from behind the bar when no one else is present. Dennis said that he has heard this vocalization several times, but after investigating the area, he found no one in sight and the door locked. Dennis also heard a rapping noise on the window near the bar when it was closed. (The first experiences were persuasive, but this last experience made a believer out of him!) Juanita has heard someone saying her name. Thinking it was Dennis beckoning her, she went around to the bar only to discover he could not have beckoned her because he was not there, nor was anyone else.

The Inn's restaurant, the Jerome Grille, is not without its share of hauntings. Glasses tend to fall off the table when no one is around to be held responsible. Staff actually witnessed a glass on the countertop slide across the surface *by itself* and crash to the floor.

While one of the cooks was bending over to grab something underneath the prep table, two plastic containers on the top shelf fell, hitting him in the back of the head. He was alone in the kitchen, and visibly shaken by the incident (luckily, the containers were plastic).

Early one morning before opening, a waitress and cook heard someone whistling. A waitress in the restroom, although she did not hear whistling, heard a female voice singing and then a loud bang. Assuming the cook had the radio going full blast, she entered the kitchen and realized that the radio was *not* on and the cook had not dropped anything to make the sound she had heard, nor had the cook heard the singing or the bang. Keep in mind that the building's reinforced eighteen-inch concrete walls hamper normal acoustics; sound does not travel much! So even if someone had been whistling, singing or playing the radio, it is not likely that people in different rooms would have heard these sounds.

Other unearthly occurrences happen throughout the Inn. Radios and water faucets turn off and on of their own volition. Laughter and voices can be heard coming from empty rooms and hallways. Guests often find that their personal items have somehow been moved from where they left them. Some of the halls and rooms have cold spots as well. There is a light in the hallway that can only be turned on or off by rotating the bulb itself (a fact guests would be unaware of), and it consistently turns itself on in the middle of the night, sometimes flashing through the transoms and disturbing guests. A cherub statue located on the dividing wall between the parlor and stairway has been observed turning when there was no one anywhere near it to make it move.

After considering all the hauntings here, I noted to Juanita that there seemed to be many ghost cats in the old hotels of Jerome. She smiled and agreed. She stated that she had never seen many cats on the streets of Jerome. Perhaps a few of them are spending their tenth lives in the comforts of the Inn at Jerome.

Address: 309 Main Street, Jerome, AZ 86331
Phone: 928-634-5094; Toll Free: 800-634-5094
Email: innatjerome@sedona.net
Website: www.innatjerome.com
Contact: Juanita & Dennis Schuyler, general managers
Lodging: 8 guest rooms
Amenities: individually stylized theme rooms: 2 with private baths, 6 with shared, terry robes, TV, AC, ceiling fans, restaurant, full-service bar

Jerome Grand Hotel

Jerome

History

The last major building constructed in Jerome, as well as one of the tallest, this huge reinforced concrete structure towers high above the town of Jerome on a 50-degree mountain slope. Five levels high and 30,000 square feet, the Spanish Mission style building began as the United Verde Hospital. It opened in 1927, and by 1930 it had become one of the most modern and best-equipped hospitals in Arizona. An additional "story"–the roof-top deck and a balcony–was added in 1929. The basement still boasts the original Kewanee boiling system which continues to heat the building today.

As Jerome's mines began to close, the population dwindled, and as the population decreased, the hospital closed. It shut down in 1950 but was kept on standby conditions, becoming an "on-call" facility in case a major tragedy or viral outbreak occurred, until the town was virtually deserted and the hospital ceased to function altogether. After the building, like the town, had lain dormant for years, the building was leased from the Phelps Dodge Corporation. In 1994, Phelps Dodge sold the building to current owner Larry Altherr and renovations began. The old Otis elevator, which once carried patients to the operating room, was repaired along with the original Kewanee Steam Boiler. Larry and his brother did the majority of the restorations, with occasional help from a pair or two of friendly helping hands. Two years later, after much patience and toil, it opened as the Jerome Grand Hotel. The elevator now transports guests up to their floor, and the boiler keeps them warm. More rooms are "on the mend," steadily being restored for future guests.

The hotel's main entrance is located in the former emergency entrance room area, and just inside the doors, you will find yourself outside the "asylum"–Asylum Restaurant and Lounge. The guest rooms have been "revived" and given an airy, country kind of feeling. From the balcony, you have breathtaking views of the Sedona Red Rocks, Verde Valley and the San Francisco Peaks. And after the sun sets in the evening, the entire outside of the hotel is lit up like Christmas and can be seen for miles, perched atop one of Jerome's highest hills. What better place for ghosts to be than a hospital, in a former ghost town?

Ghosts

The most famous and mysterious ghost of the Jerome Grand Hotel is a former hospital maintenance man named Claude Harvey. In April of 1935, Mr. Harvey was found dead in the basement after one of his daily treks to service the elevator and three boilers. He apparently died instantly when his head was pinned underneath the elevator. A hospital employee discovered the body approximately twenty minutes after Mr. Harvey left to repair an alleged elevator malfunction. There were no witnesses to this "accident," however, and his death has remained very much a mystery. Some believe that Mr. Harvey was murdered. The electrical engineer testified that the elevator was in perfect working order. Larry Altherr disclosed something to us related to the incident that he discovered during renovations: the only way such a malfunction could have occurred was through deliberate tampering. Someone would had to have hot-wired around a safety switch, called the Reverse Phase Safety Switch, which was in perfect working order when Altherr acquired the hotel. Despite this, during renovations, he found the switch bypassed–still hot-wired (he corrected the problem). This provocative evidence indicates that Claude Harvey's death was deliberately orchestrated, a result of foul play. It appears that he *was* murdered!

Many believe that Claude Harvey's ghost does not rest in peace, as a short shadowy figure of a man is often seen lingering in the hallways and boiler room. There are also mysterious lights that appear in the elevator shaft. The small balls of light (orbs) have actually been seen with the naked eye inside the shaft. Sounds of the creaking elevator sometimes echo throughout the building, even though the elevator is parked on the top floor and not in service.

Team member Megan Taylor and I had the pleasure of meeting LaWanda, one of the afternoon desk clerks. While she was a little hesitant at first, she shared several scary experiences of her own. She interprets her encounters in a positive way, though, feeling that the spirits like to interact with her.

LaWanda told us about a confrontation she had with ghosts on a day she was wearing shoes with decorative buckles. These particular shoe buckles were not easy to undo. When she sat down at the front desk, the buckles were in place. But when she glanced down at her shoes later, she discovered that someone or something had unfastened the buckles.

Since she began living in the hotel, LaWanda has also had several visits from a ghost cat in her room. What's more, she has felt it jump up on to her bed.

When she was working as a housekeeper, at times LaWanda felt someone sneak up and stand behind her. The presence only remained there for seconds. She could feel something, even though she never saw anybody when she looked. Sometimes it would even touch her.

Another desk clerk has heard noises coming from the gift shop. She was alarmed and went to inspect what had made such a racket in the quiet of night. The sounds had been created by items falling off the shelf. Evidently, "someone" was knocking things off the shelves; she found small dolls and trinkets scattered along the floor.

One evening, the same desk clerk also saw the shadowy outline of a man standing at the foot of the stairs. He stood there, motionless, and gazed in her direction, seeming to watch her from the stairs as she read. She could not make out his features, and after a few minutes, he faded away.

The upper levels of the Jerome Grand have fostered hordes of encounters with the paranormal. A guest on the second floor saw a lady's face peering in through her second-story window. Many guests on the third floor smell cigarette and cigar smoke in the non-smoking rooms. Some have smelled whiskey as well.

Team member Shiela McCurdy and I smelled ether as we investigated the third floor hallway. This unusual odor was appropriate to the location: the hospital's operating rooms were on the third floor.

When a former employee was assigned housekeeping duties on the third floor, she began to have intense night-mares. These nightmares continued during the entire time she was employed at the hotel. They ceased after she resigned.

Many guests hear voices coming from unoccupied rooms on the third floor. These voices can be heard conversing from various places, especially Rooms 31, 33, 39A and 39B.

The fourth floor was the maternity ward for the hospital. Here guests and housekeeping have witnessed balls of color-ful lights floating in midair. These lights have been blue and white in color and often sparkle as they disappear. Some feel these orbs are the spirits of mothers and babies peacefully marking their presence. Although there were many deaths in the hospital, many lives began here as well.

On the fourth floor, a guest saw a man's face in the mirror of her room. The lady only caught the face staring back at her for a few seconds before it vanished in the blink of an eye. She was the lone guest in the room. (Spirits will often appear in mirrors as you are gazing into them.)

Many unsettling echoes resound throughout the Jerome Grand. There are footsteps heard throughout the hotel. Squeaky wheels of old hospital carts creak down the halls. Doors open and shut, lights go on and off and the shadowy figures of doctors brush past you as they hurry down the hall to the third floor operating room.

A good friend of mine, George Sarrat, recently shared a

Does this orb reflect the spirit of someone who was a patient?
(Photo by Robyn Abels)

paranormal adventure of his own that he had while staying at the Jerome Grand. He was enjoying a cocktail in the Asylum Lounge and got up to go to the restroom. As he walked into the hallway toward the facilities, he experienced a psychic vision flash that lasted several seconds. What he "saw" was a room full of people—doctors, nurses and patients hustling around in what looked like an emergency room. He later talked to Nancy Smith, the night desk clerk, who confirmed that he had indeed been in the old emergency room area of the hospital. It seems that he witnessed past traumas being received.

When you spend a night at the Jerome Grand Hotel, it may not be a very restful experience, but it is likely to be a memorable one! You could witness and hear many grim things, such as the sounds of coughing and moaning from patients of the past. But never fear, most likely a ghostly nurse in a crisp white uniform dress and cap will be there to attend to them!

Address: 200 Hill Street, P.O. Box H, Jerome, AZ 86331
Phone: 928-634-8200
Fax: 928-639-0299
Email: hotel@wildapache.net
Website: www.jeromegrandhotel.com
Contact: Larry Altherr, owner
Lodging: 22 rooms with private baths
Amenities: TV, ATM, restaurant, lounge, gift shop

The Surgeon's House Bed & Breakfast
Jerome

History

The United Verde Copper Company built this beautiful Mediterranean-style mansion in 1916. As the chief surgeon's residence for the town hospital located next door, all the modern comforts were included in this spacious 4,000 square foot home. The Surgeon's House was designed by Los Angeles architect Arthur Kelly to have a smashing view of the Verde Valley and downtown Jerome. Included in the design were live-in maid's quarters and a chauffeur's cottage in the back.

The next residents were Dr. Arthur Carlson, his wife Maude, and their children. They enjoyed a busy social life and loved to entertain guests in the elegance of their home. In the late 1920s and early 1930s, between inhabitants Dr. Kaull and Dr. Carlson, the mansion also functioned as a nurses' residence.

When Jerome's mines closed in 1953, a mass exodus occurred in the once prosperous town, and the house gradually fell into a state of disrepair. The mansion was added to the National Historic Registry in 1966, and through the years, has been home to councilmen, the mayor, geologists and the town's postmaster, among others. In recent years, owner Andrea Prince has restored the mansion to its original style and grace and transformed it into a relaxing and artful Bed and Breakfast accented by lavish gardens.

Ghosts

Although its current owner does not relish the idea of her home being considered haunted, it seems that spirits have lingered in this house for a long time. They belong here because it was once their home, too.

It may be that a ghost resident named Alice was the former housekeeper of the home that once stood next to the Surgeon's House. Some of the guests have reported encountering Alice–always in the same blue clothing–in the Maid's Suite Front (now a guest room). Some speculate that Alice has taken on the maid's job at the grand old Bed and Breakfast to make sure that today's guests are comfortable and feel at peace. At the same time, Alice can also keep a watchful eye on the empty lot where the house of her employer once stood.

One momentous night, Andrea awoke and witnessed the spirit of a man in a suit, holding a briefcase that somewhat resembled a doctor's bag, walk across her master bedroom toward where she was sleeping. He walked into the bathroom, changed into his pajamas and then slipped into her bed. It startled her (to say the least), and the next thing she knew, he was gone!

Other guests staying in the Master Suite have watched as an enchanted couple danced together for several minutes. Imagine watching a movie that repeats the same frame over and over and gradually fades out. Could it be that these are the ghosts of Dr. and Mrs. Carlson entertaining guests in their home once again?

Team member Megan Taylor and I had our own ghostly experience when we visited the Surgeon's House. As we approached the house, we opened the gate, being careful to leave it partially open, about twelve inches. We knocked on the door but the innkeeper was out doing errands for her upcoming guests, we peeked in the windows and were awed by the wonderful decorating. As we headed back down the stairs, we were surprised to find the gate shut and the latch closed. There had been no wind to blow it shut. There was no spring catch to pull it. And we had not been far away; we should have heard the wrought iron gate clang if it had closed itself. Perhaps it was Alice doing her job, protecting the home and neighborhood she regards so dearly.

Address:	101 Hill Street, P.O. Box 998, Jerome, AZ 86331
Phone:	928-639-1452; Toll Free: 800-639-1452
Email:	surgehouse1@wildapache.net
Website:	www.surgeonshouse.com
Contact:	Andrea Prince, owner
Lodging:	4 suites
Amenities:	TV, radio, alarm clock, common living room, dining room, atrium, lush gardens, hot tub, fireplace

H--t l ru..swi- (

Kingman

History

Built in 1909, Hotel Brunswick was one of the first three-story buildings in the area and was completely unique in status and the quality of service it offered. The original owners, Irishmen John Mulligan and Thompson (whose first name is unknown), earned themselves quite a reputation in the area with the classy accommodations and amenities they provided, such as Waterford crystal stemware and solid brass beds, as well as electricity and phones (state of the art offerings for the era, to be sure!).

A romantic drama ensued after Mulligan and Thompson each fell in love with the same woman. Inevitably, tensions in the love triangle mounted, driving a rift between the two partners that resulted in a one-of-a-kind division of property in 1912: A wall was constructed to divide the two hotels; instead of one hotel, now there were two. Of the two separate hotels coexisting within the same building, one side, belonging to Mulligan, featured the bar and 25 rooms, and the other half, with the restaurant and other 25 rooms, fell to Thompson. (The object of their dueling affections, Sarah, eventually selected and married Mulligan. She died of an ongoing illness years later and is believed to be one of the Brunswick ghosts.)

This eccentric business arrangement continued until the 1960s when Joe Artero bought both sides and tore down the wall. The interesting thing about the two partners was that they understood marketing; even though they had a falling out and divided the hotel, the name of the establishment never changed and business, for both men, was good.

Gerard J. Guedon, the hotel's latest proprietor, has done extensive renovations to bring Hotel Brunswick back to its former glory. It offers much in the way of hospitality, ghosts and rustic, turn-of-the-century Southwestern charm.

Ghosts

One of the first experiences Gerard had with the Brunswick spirits happened shortly after he purchased the hotel. When his girlfriend came downstairs into the lobby for morning coffee, he noticed a yellow mark on her neck. He mentioned it to her, and then she laughed and pointed out that he had one on his neck, too. They went upstairs to check her daughter's neck but found that she was unmarked. The marks came off easily, and they all had a good laugh. Gerard later noted that they felt like the experience had been some kind of test.

Gerard was tested again in Room 312. Every time he entered the room, something caused his hair to stand on end (the magnetic energy that a ghost produces feels like cold electricity). Eventually, this, coupled with the ghosts' repeated pranks, caused him to lose his French temper (Gerard is from Beaufort, France). He went back into the room, sat down and had a chat with whatever was causing his discomfort. He stated, "Look, I just moved here. I've spent my money. You leave or we'll both go crazy." They apparently came to an understanding that day. Since then, the ghost has left Gerard alone and instead of an antagonist, has become something of a helping force (or business "partner").

A German couple who stayed in Room 201 in 2002 (a couple of years after Gerard obtained ownership) had their own brush with the Brunswick's prankster. When they came downstairs in the morning, they told Gerard that the hotel had a ghost. The woman explained with great excitement that something grabbed her leg and tried to pull her out of the bed! Her husband apparently woke up and witnessed this happening, but all he saw was her leg sticking straight out of the bed as if someone was tugging at it. (Perhaps she had asked the question, "Is this place haunted?" and the ghost responded by "pulling her leg.")

At some point after he purchased the hotel, an old pipe burst in one of the bathrooms, causing flooding and some moderate water damage. After it was repaired, Gerard thought he had solved his plumbing problems, but he was mistaken. He woke up another night to hear a funny hissing noise. Getting out of bed, he went into the bathroom where the noise seemed to be coming from and found a pinhole-sized leak in one of the fixtures. He shut off the water immediately, and the next day he called a plumber to come and replace all of the fixtures so there would be no more plumbing problems. Gerard feels that the ghost was trying to warn him about the serious impending plumbing disaster. Such a small hole does not make a loud hissing sound, but to him, its sound was clearly audible—the same volume up close as it was when he was laying in bed—an impossibility. Bearing in mind that upwards of 100 trains per day pass through Kingman, the noise interference, sound amplification and timing of his waking all point to ghosts giving Gerard help from beyond to prevent another costly accident.

As for the identities of the Brunswick's ghosts, Gerard knows that one guest died in the hotel in the 1930s. Sarah, the object of Mulligan and Thompson's desire, also died here. One of the housekeepers feels sure there are spirits because she can feel them as she works. She feels strongly that they are friendly, not malevolent spirits.

Gerard confessed to ghost hunter Megan Taylor and me that he didn't realize how expensive the remodeling and renovating would be when he purchased the hotel, and had spent approximately twice the amount of money he had originally intended. Concerned over finances, he was venting out loud to himself one evening. The next morning when he came downstairs, he found several old pennies—whose dates went way back—stacked upon the bar, in addition to some old pennies that turned up in the east corridors of the second and third floors. This did not make much sense to Gerard because everything in the bar is charged in $.25 or $.50 increments, and pennies are not used, even to make change. There seemed to be no reason for pennies to be stacked around the hotel. He instructed the bartenders to make sure the bar was cleaned off and all change locked up each night when they closed, but the pennies continued to appear–not every night, but randomly off and on for several weeks. Gerard believes this was a show of support and acceptance, as well as a sign from the Brunswick spirits that more prosperous times were around the corner. And so they were!

Author's Note:

Often when you move to a haunted location, the spirits know you are moving in on THEIR turf. They will test you by hiding things, flicking lights on and off, moving objects and so on. The ghosts in my house tested me by knocking over my doll collection, ruining home improvement projects and popping light bulbs. They do not like change. So Gerard's ghosts were testing his mental courage with pranks: at first you think you are going crazy before you realize that the strange occurrences are caused by ghosts. They were also testing his patience until he put his foot down. In essence, he was letting them know that it was HIS property and they were welcome only as long as they learned to peacefully coexist.

Address:	315 East Andy Devine, Route 66, Kingman, AZ 86401
Phone:	928-718-1800
Fax:	928-718-1801
Email:	rsvp@hotel-brunswick.com
Website:	www.hotel-brunswick.com
Contact:	Gerard J. Guedon, owner
Lodging:	24 guest rooms and suites: 19 with private baths and 5 with shared
Amenities:	cable TV, AC, Internet access (data ports on phone lines and local access), restaurant, bar, Amtrak transfers, complimentary continental breakfast, pet-friendly establishment, laundry and dry-cleaning service, library, business center, sitting room

Oatman Hotel
Oatman

History

The Oatman Hotel sits in one of the West's old gold mining ghost towns in the western foothills of the Black Mountains, off old U.S. Route 66. Originally built in 1902, it was rebuilt during 1924 after a major fire swept through the town, destroying all main buildings. At first named the Durlin Hotel, this two-story adobe building became the Oatman Hotel in the 1960s and is particularly noteworthy for its Mission/Spanish Revival architecture. The structure has been listed on the National Register of Historic Buildings since 1983.

One of the Oatman's traditions pays homage to its former patrons: the walls and ceilings of the bar and restaurant are lined with dollar bills signed and dated by miners who were in Oatman looking to make their fortunes in gold. When these gold-mining hopefuls had an extra greenback or two, gold-hearted Anna Eder, the operator of the then-titled "Eder Café," allowed men to post the marked bills for a rainy day, when fortune wasn't smiling on them so warmly. And if the mines happened to fail and they became broke, they still had at least one more beer coming.

The Oatman Hotel is the famous honeymoon spot where Clark Gable and Carole Lombard spent their wedding night on March 29, 1939, after tying the knot in Kingman, Arizona, just up the road a piece. Although many establishments like to claim that Gable and Lombard stayed overnight there, it is a documented fact that the newlyweds made it as far as Oatman on the way back to Hollywood before they pulled over here for the night. The couple used to return to Oatman to rejuvenate away from the rat race in the desert's open tranquility; in fact, Gable is well regarded here for having played poker with the locals. Room 15, the room where the famous duo bedded down for the night, is an available guest room.

Of all the ghosts present, the most active and famous ghost in the hotel is "Oatie." Oatie's real name was William Ray Flour; William was an Irishman who emigrated to America in pursuit of the American Dream, seeking to make his fortune. He ended up working in the gold mines in and around Oatman, working hard to save his money so that he could someday pay for his wife and two children back in Ireland to cross the ocean and continent separating them, hoping one day to again be a family. It is known that William was a boarder in the Oatman Hotel, although the exact dates of his residence there are uncertain.

William, like many miners of the day separated from family, drank very heavily. And when tragedy struck, William's drinking became desperately excessive—more so than ever before. In a cruel turn of Fortune's wheel, his family never made it to this country; all three family members perished during the voyage (the details of their deaths are unknown). Unhappy and cantankerous, spinning out of control, William became the notorious town drunk. Townspeople speculated that his grief led him to drink himself to death as he turned to the bottle for comfort. William died, cold and alone, on a 1930 winter's night in the alley behind the hotel. He had been walking home from a bar, sat down beside a trash heap in the back and passed out—nothing necessarily out of the ordinary for him—except this time, he never came to. William's body lay where it fell, undiscovered for two days. Town legend states that a group of his old cronies dug a hole in the alley and buried him in the same spot where he died in a shallow, unmarked grave.

Ghosts

Ghost hunter Megan Taylor and I located hotel manager Suzie Clark in the restaurant where she warmly greeted us. Suzie led the way upstairs to the Gable and Lombard Room, letting us in so we could (hopefully) document any paranormal activity. We were able to photograph orbs using our digital cameras, and our EMF meter showed a high reading just inside the doorway. Suzie related that employees and guests alike have heard laughter and whispering coming from this honeymoon suite. One spirit photographer definitively photographed a man's ghost in the room while others have succeeded in photographing ecto mists, or swirling, vaporous clouds of spirit matter.

Once-upon-a-time honeymooner or deceased miner?

In spite of his sad life, Oatie the ghost is a prankster. You can hear him laughing intermittently throughout the hotel, and he has been known to play his bagpipes during the night. The old jukebox that used to be in the lobby would sometimes start up by itself.

Oatie also frequents the gift shop. He apparently had taken a liking to a certain doll on display because he enjoyed moving it about the shop. At times, guests and employees would see it hurtling through the air until one day, the doll was finally sold. Oatie searched for "his" doll high and low during the night, ransacking the entire gift shop in the process. Although he didn't find it, he did find a suitable replacement that he played with instead.

Oatie also likes to play tricks on the guests who stay in his room (a room marked "Oatie's Room"). One guest complained that this room was icy cold on a day when the outside temperature was 105 degrees or more. A different guest reported that the room's doorknob turned by itself several times during his stay. Yet another guest reported hearing footsteps in the room and the room (again) turning very cold.

Oatie's abrupt appearances have alarmed many guests, causing them to frantically check out in the middle of the night. Housekeepers report that, after preparing the rooms for guests, they have, on occasion, discovered their efforts were for naught during their final room check. Even though nobody else was on the floor, they have discovered every guest bed in an unmade mess. Who do they blame for making them work even harder? Oatie. Every time.

Suzie senses that Oatie is a lonely spirit who just wants people to acknowledge him. She believes that he comes into her room as well and moves objects around while he's visiting. She also believes that he is partial to women and has even been responsible for goosing a few. Take, for example, this surprise ghost experience that Suzie shared about one of the waitresses: While cleaning the bar after hours, this waitress felt an invisible hand slap her on the rear end!

Megan and I were lucky to sit down with a couple of Oatman regulars (true town characters) to hear their stories about Oatie's attention-getting tactics. We bellied up to the bar and began to chat with a gentleman who told us stories of ashtrays sliding down the bar. He also pointed out where glasses repeatedly fall off a particular shelf behind the bar, even though it's lined with rubber shelf-lining to keep them from moving. Even though they move around and fall off, he said that none of the glasses has ever been broken. And sometimes, the glasses are found stacked on the floor instead of the shelves.

This same gentleman also spent some time as a resident of the Oatman Hotel in Room 18 and shared this anecdote about his first experience in the room: After he rented the room, he went upstairs to look it over. As soon as he stepped inside, the door slammed behind him and locked, and he had to use his pocketknife to lift the locking mechanism. Thinking the hotel staff was playing a joke on him, he stepped out into the hallway, expecting to see one or two employees having a laugh at his expense, but he saw no one. Puzzled, he stepped back into his room whereupon the door slammed behind him and locked him in again.

Perhaps it was just Oatie playing another prank on one of his friends–the guests and staff of the Oatman Hotel–the pot of gold he still calls home.

Address: 181 Main Street, Route 66, Oatman, AZ 86433
Phone: 928-768-4408
Fax: 928-788-2425
Contact: Suzie Clark, manager
Lodging: 10 rooms
Amenities: restaurant and saloon

Grand Canyon Caverns Inn
Peach Springs

History

The Grand Canyon Caverns Inn is located on historic Route 66 between Kingman and Seligman. Although it is a separate entity from the Grand Canyon National Park and is not affiliated with the National Park Service, the Grand Canyon Caverns has been a stopping point for hikers of nearby Havasu Canyon for over thirty-seven years. The Inn was built near the entrance to the Caverns, not far from where the building housing the restaurant and curio shop is located. The natural limestone caverns are accessed by means of an elevator that descends 210 feet underground, or roughly 21 stories. They were discovered in 1927, quite by accident.

One evening, as a young cowboy and woodcutter named Walter Peck was on his way to play poker with his friends, he nearly fell into a large, funnel-shaped hole. Not properly equipped to investigate his discovery, he continued on to the poker game where he told his buddies about the new, gaping hole in his well-traveled path. So the next day, equipped with ropes and lanterns, Walter returned with his fellow cowboys, ready to explore the chasm. One of the members of this spelunking expedition (not Walter) was secured to a rope and lowered into the depths of the fissure. When he finally reached the bottom, the brave cowboy began to explore his surroundings, using a lantern to light his way. His light eventually shone on what he thought was a vein of gold. Eagerly gathering a sackful of samples–thinking they had struck it rich–he tugged on the rope to be hauled back up and was lifted out. After showing his companions the metal fragments, he reported to Walter and his other companions that he had also seen two human skeletons and the remains of a horse saddle fifty feet down. When the assay report (the metallurgical chemical analysis) came back, however, they found out that the samples they had retrieved and sent in were not gold at all–only lots of iron oxide, or rust.

Since he had already bought the land, Walter came up with a new idea so that his investment was not a complete bust. He began to charge a fee–twenty-five cents–for the brave and the curious to enter his property to see the skeletons (which, by this time, had been transformed by the media into the remains of cavemen), and he built a very "primitive" elevator whereby visitors were tied to one end of a rope and lowered down by a hand-cranked winch. In 1935, the Civilian Conservation Corps built a new entrance to the Caverns with a wooden staircase, three ladders and a sixty-foot swinging bridge, which was the only way to access the Caverns until 1962, when the modern-day elevator was installed and the natural entrance sealed.

Ghosts

The restaurant, curio shop and Caverns are all allegedly haunted by the ghost of founder Walter Peck. Ghost hunter Megan Taylor and I met with Jackie, the manager of the curio shop, and she told us that sometimes, when she is working late in the office, she hears the elevator going up and down into the Caverns even though the place is empty and the elevator is supposed to be off. She and several guests have also noticed that the light fixtures in the restaurant shake and swing back and forth at odd hours of the day and night.

Roxanna, an employee who works in the restaurant, has also heard the elevator going up and down the shaft when it has been shut down for the night. She added that she has noticed the elevator and cavern lights turning on and off on their own. Several times, she has heard furniture being moved around in the restaurant as well. When she would enter the dining room to check what was happening, she always found everything situated as it was when she left, in its rightful place. In addition to this, Roxanna has heard voices of "people" talking in the restaurant after closing, and when she has gone to investigate, no guests (or anyone else visible!) have been present.

The Caverns were once a Native American burial site (see the Caverns web site) and the bones found there were actually the remains of two Hualapai brothers who died in a flu epidemic. Jackie believes these spirits could also be haunting the area. Although the bones were moved many years ago, their spirits may still be lingering in the Caverns.

Some guests at the Caverns have felt a strange presence close by and, soon after, noticed someone—an additional person who had not been in the group when the tour began—riding in the elevator or exploring with them. When they again looked for the imposter, the "person" was gone!

The ghosts also play with the ovens in the kitchen, adjusting their temperatures or turning them off altogether. When alone working late, Roxanna has felt a spirit brush against her. She feels that the ghosts are just practical jokers. Perhaps they are the spirits of Walter Peck and his cowboy pals preparing for another late night poker game!

Address: P.O. Box 180, Route 66, Peach Springs, AZ
              86434
Phone: 928-422-4565
Fax: 928-422-4470
Email: reservations@grandcanyoncaverns.com
Website: www.grandcanyoncaverns.com
Contact: Coni Abelon, hospitality coordinator
Lodging: 48 rooms
Amenities: AC, TV, laundry room, convenience market,
              outdoor swimming pool, cavern tours every half
              hour—every day except Christmas Day

Hotel San Carlos
Phoenix

History

Hotel San Carlos opened in 1928 as one of the most modern hotels in the Southwest. Financed by the Dwight B. Heard Investment Company, it was one of Phoenix's first high-rise buildings: seven stories with 175 luxurious rooms, which offered circulating ice water and air conditioning and could be accessed using attendant-operated elevators (the first in the city). Each pedestal sink had three spigots—for hot, cold and ice-cold water—some of which remain in the hotel today. The hotel was built to appeal to the city's growing tourist industry and provided an ideal mixing location for the rich and famous and the Phoenix elite. Celebrities such as Mae West, Clark Gable, Carole Lombard, Ingrid Bergman, Marilyn Monroe and Spencer Tracy were former patrons of the hotel.

A water well—still operating in the basement, still supplying icy cold water—was dug on the property in 1874 when the city's first schoolhouse was built on the site. Unbeknownst to the well-diggers, they had tapped into a spring that legend says had been considered sacred by Native Americans for hundreds of years. This is where a source of the hauntings could be centered; it is known that an open well is a conduit for ghost activity.

The original one-story adobe schoolhouse built in 1874– the first Phoenix school–was replaced in 1879 by a four-room brick schoolhouse, used until it was condemned in 1916 because it was literally falling apart. Although the property– the entire block–was sold with plans to develop a nine-story, 300-room hotel, the project was never realized. Hotel San Carlos was finally erected, filling the void on Central Avenue in its own first-rate, regal way.

The building is decorated in an Italian Renaissance style. The lobby has high, molded ceilings, terrazzo marble floors, and chandeliers of Austrian crystal. The elevators have copper doors, and one of the manual elevators still conducts guests to their rooms. Most of the hotel's original woodwork has been preserved along with the rest of its architectural finery. All of the managements' preservation efforts through the years have helped to make it a member of the Historic Hotels of America–the only establishment in downtown Phoenix able to make such a claim.

Ghosts

Although the schoolhouse was abandoned in 1916, for some "children," school is still in session. Whispers from the demolished schoolhouse still linger throughout the halls. The ghosts of three young boys have been heard running through the hallways of the hotel (they were especially active during the renovations of 2002). On several occasions, guests have complained about unexplainable laughter reverberating as children run down the halls–unexplainable because these reports have come when no children are registered. I have photographed three orbs in one of the hallways that I can only assume are the three schoolboys. Their ghosts supposedly reside in the basement of the hotel. (Interestingly, the hotel's elevators often descend to the basement no matter what button is pushed.)

Arizona Paranormal Investigations conducted a spirit

workshop at the San Carlos in February of 2002. While at the mid-level laundry room, a large volume of hot air poured out into the hallway. The room had been cold just prior to the blast of heat (no laundry had been done in it for at least twelve hours). When the heat hit, the team was sitting directly across from the laundry room, about six feet away, and they were nearly overcome by the blast, which lasted about fifteen seconds. Their psychics entered the room, felt the heat and sensed that there had been a fire in the room that may have claimed someone's life.

The major ghost of the San Carlos is Miss Leone Jensen. Leone was despondent over ill health following a nervous breakdown; she had come to Phoenix to see doctors for a serious ongoing lung condition. The attractive blond had been staying in a room on the third floor and had only been there for two days when on May 7, 1928, she climbed the seventh floor staircase to the roof. From there, she leaped to her death.

I found an article written in *The Arizona Republic* dated May 8, 1928, that described some of the mystery woman's last hours. She was fully dressed, wearing a lightweight, tan-colored summer coat with a hat to match. She also wore a thin rose-colored dress, light shoes and stockings. Investigators said the twenty-five-year-old jumped at about 3:00 a.m. It was believed she held her hat and purse in her hands as she hurtled through the air, landing on the corner of Monroe and Central Avenue.

Leone left three suicide notes. One noted that the severity of her illness was more than she could endure:

> *My burden was more than I could carry, so I am coming 'back home' in the way I predicted, but not as a suicide. But this long agony is too much for me and now having suffered a nervous breakdown, I could never go through with it. I am too weak to walk and all in all, I am through.*

She apparently changed her mind about her ability to end her life as her anguish increased. Another letter was addressed to a Los Angeles undertaker with several last requests regarding her funeral arrangements, and the third was to the hotel manager, instructing him where to send her belongings.

Leone's suicidal experience could be the reason that she still roams the hallways of Hotel San Carlos. There is a theory that if a ghost was Christian while alive, then the person's fear of hell may keep them behind, in limbo, if they have taken their own life.

Guests have reported seeing the cloudy white figure of a woman walking the hallways–hallways where they feel breezes and cold spots they cannot explain. Some hear an uncanny moaning noise.

We felt a cold chill in the area near the staircase on the 7th floor where Leone must have paced back and forth, glancing out the window before making her final ascent to the hotel roof. While standing outside the San Carlos, I photographed a large orb near the ground, on Monroe Street.

This is a quietly eerie building where, on occasion, you can hear the laughter and whispers of carefree children echoing in the empty rooms.

Address: 202 North Central Avenue, Phoenix, AZ 85004
Phone: 602-253-4121; Toll Free: 866-253-4121
Fax: 602-253-6721
Email: info@hotelsancarlos.com
Website: www.hotelsancarlos.com
Contact: Bruce Barnes, general manager
Lodging: 121 rooms and 11 celebrity suites
Amenities: private baths, cable TV, phone data ports, coffee makers with gourmet coffee, clock radios, pool, continental breakfast, 3 restaurants, gift shop, barber shop, shoe shine shop

Hassayampa Inn
Prescott

History

The Hassayampa Inn was built during 1927 in Prescott, which became Arizona's first territorial capital in 1864. Since many of Prescott's first settlers were from the East and Midwest, residents resisted the region's favored Pueblo Revival style when designing their town buildings. The four-story Hassayampa Inn, named after a nearby river, is a good example of the characteristic Midwestern design found here. It has an exterior of red brick trimmed in white and its own bell tower. It also has a place on the National Register of Historic Places and is a member of the National Trust Historic Hotels of America, a group that recognizes outstanding preservation efforts.

The hotel was built for summer tourists from the Phoenix area who sought an escape from the desert heat in Prescott's temperate mountain climate. Money was raised through public subscription to build this hotel near Courthouse Plaza—

one of the focal points of Prescott where the historic buildings of infamous Whiskey Row are situated. Shares were offered to the public at $1 to $20.

The interior of the hotel is a compromise between Midwestern design and a touch of Southwestern Territorial flavor. Just adjacent to the building in another historical structure, a restoration project is underway that, when finished, will provide guests with a grand ballroom and even more outdoor gardens. Upgraded and refurbished in 2002, the Inn offers handsome, refined surroundings indoors and out, with charm, cozy atmosphere and class. Don't miss the rooftop terrace overlooking downtown Prescott.

Famous Silent Screen Western movie star, Tom Mix, often stayed at the Hassayampa Inn when filming in the area. For Mix and other movie cowboys, this was the only place to stay in Prescott because it was the only place that catered to elite clientele. Guests from years past evidently enjoyed their stays so much that they have decided to take up permanent residence. These ghosts have already attracted considerable public interest; the Discovery Channel spent two weeks documenting the phenomena of ghost appearances at the Hassayampa Inn in the summer of 2003.

Ghosts

When I arrived, I was taken down to the basement of the Inn where I spoke with the housekeeping supervisor. She immediately announced that none of the housekeeping staff likes to work on the fourth floor. I couldn't wait to hear more!

She related that her daughter and a friend had decided to spend the night in Room 402. Before bed, the girls secured three locks and placed a "Do Not Disturb" sign on the outside of the door. They woke up twice to find the door unlocked and the sign back on the inside.

Not wanting the glare of morning sunlight to filter in from the room's east windows at dawn, the girls tucked the chair up tight against the curtains to hold them against the window. They also wanted the bathroom light to be on, but with the door shut, so before bed, they made sure to close it. In the morning, they awoke to brightness streaming into the room. Something had raised the curtain ten inches above the chair during the night and pushed the bathroom door wide open. As soon as they saw the door ajar, they placed their heavy purses up against the door, then watched as it began inching open, little by little.

One summer, a young man who was staying with his girlfriend in Room 426 woke up in the middle of the night. He had the eerie sensation that someone was in the room with them. Though he managed to fall back asleep, he awoke later to a presence hugging him. His girlfriend remained oblivious the entire time, asleep on the other side of the bed.

Two unrelated incidents illustrate other types of paranormal activity common to Room 426. After an entire night of lights switching themselves on and off, a guest became so frustrated that she unscrewed all the light bulbs from their fixtures. Another couple experienced the lights *and* TV turning off and on in the middle of the night. Then in the morning, to top it all off, they found their toothbrushes were missing!

Perhaps now you can see why housekeepers have grown reluctant to work in the vicinity of this haunted room.

Kitchen staff have reported a child apparition who frequents the kitchen and causes some innocent trouble on his visits (these visits are accompanied by the sound of a small child's footsteps). When the spirit first began to come around, they observed bizarre episodes in which all the gas burners would shut off simultaneously. Over time, they have learned to detect the presence, and this awareness helps alert them when the burners are about to be extinguished.

A bellman at the hotel told me this spooky anecdote: Sometime during the course of an otherwise inconsequential day, he had to go up to the roof to unstick the elevator. After returning downstairs, the front desk told him that a phone call had just come in on caller ID from Room 449. This news rattled him. Room 449 is no longer in existence.

I headed to the lounge to collect some more tales and learned that one of the bar regulars is a ghost. Bartender Stephanie informed me about a very tall "man," referred to as the Night Watchman by staff in all departments, who materializes in a pinstripe suit but only when the weather is warm. He typically makes a circuit, traveling from the dining room area through the bar's seating area, where he then heads for the front door. After jiggling the door, as if to make sure it is secure, the Night Watchman fades away. Many bartenders have witnessed his "last call" walk through the sitting area of the lounge at the end of the evening.

Another of the bartenders, Joseph, joined us and reflected on another strange story. A Scottish couple was seated at the bar, and the lady was wearing large, ornate earrings. She felt something brush by her right ear very lightly and responded by grabbing her earlobe, at which point she discovered that her right earring was missing. Assuming that it had fallen off, she, her husband and Joseph began to hunt for it. They found the tiny back of the earring in the small bar area, but could not recover the earring itself. Figuring it could not have rolled far, they pulled back the carpeting, checking to see if it had gotten lodged underneath it somehow. She even went into the restroom to check her clothing. It was never found.

Rather than work with ghosts, many people resign their jobs. This was the scenario that played out for Shawna, a new lady bartender, when bottles fell at her feet and broke. For no apparent reason, the normally sturdy shelf tipped and the bottles fell. Seeing secure shelves tip and empty their contents onto the floor was enough for Shawna. She quit that very moment.

Legend has it that shortly after the Hassayampa Inn opened in 1927, a honeymoon couple checked into Room 426. The husband left to go out for cigarettes, but never returned. His bride, Faith, kept a lonely vigil from the balcony, anticipating his arrival. But after several days of waiting, the despondent new bride gave up hope and hung herself in the room. Faith's presence still haunts the Inn.

Guests and employees alike have recounted various chilling things that indicate Faith's company. They say the TV comes on by itself, lights turn on and off and the alarm clock beeps in the middle of the night. A certain maintenance worker saw Faith at 7:00 one morning, dressed in a pink gown. He watched as she passed through the hallway, crossed in front of him and disappeared into a room–Faith's room. Other staff members have reported unexplainable cold spots or smelled fresh flowers in the empty room.

A housekeeper reported having a close encounter with Faith as well. Routinely entering the room one day, she was astonished when she saw a young woman standing at the foot of the bed, clutching a bouquet of flowers and weeping. When the housekeeper asked if she could help her, the woman grabbed her arm, then disappeared. The frightened housekeeper ran out of the room and did not return to work for several days.

A staff member standing in the hallway in front of Faith's room had her own distressing experience while holding a cup of coffee. As she was telling a friend that she wanted to see if she could do some research on Faith's story at the library, her coffee cup "jumped" and spilled coffee all over her hand. Something jostled her. It seems that Faith didn't like the idea. She canceled her trip to the library.

During my visit, I had the pleasure of staying in the most haunted room in the Inn–Faith's room. I was in Prescott on company business, and the staff knew I was working on my book project. They were anxious to see what would happen when I spent the night in Room 426.

Each time I put my key in the door, a spark of blue static would shoot out and snap at my hand. (Staff member Mardi Read reported the same experience with this blue spark shocking her during room checks.) Throughout my stay, my EMF meter registered a steady reading of 2.9 and higher in the bathroom, a high reading indicating a strong spirit presence (under normal conditions, it reads .1). At midnight, I snapped off the TV and lights and went to bed. The bed vibrated as I fell asleep.

Some extraordinary things transpired during the night. At 1:00 a.m., I woke up to find the TV back on. I again shut it off and crawled back into bed. Then I felt someone– presumably Faith–sitting at the end of the bed on the left side. I pushed her off with my left foot. She sat down in the same spot. I pushed her away once more.

At some point, I heard someone in the bathroom filling a glass with water, and then there was a presence of someone hovering over me with the glass. I laid there covering my face, expecting to get drenched, but with my fingers spread so that I could peek out and see what was going to happen. Whoever it was tipped the glass, but no water poured out on me. As soon as it tipped, it disappeared, leaving no water and no glass. It was a chilling yet thrilling moment!

Be sure to stay on the fourth floor of the Hassayampa Inn when you come to stay in Prescott. Ask for Faith's room, and perhaps the forlorn bride will share a cup of coffee with you!

Address: 122 East Gurley Street, Prescott, AZ 86301
Phone: 928-778-9434; Toll Free: 800-322-1927
Fax: 928-445-8590
Email: inn1@mindspring.com
Website: www.hassayampainn.com
Contact: Tammy Anderson, manager
Lodging: 67 rooms
Amenities: TV, phone, restaurant, lounge, meeting rooms

Hotel Vendome
Prescott

History

Hotel Vendome is a charming two-story, red brick structure built by J.B. Jones in 1917. After a woman named Mary lost her house due to back taxes, her home was leveled, making way for the Hotel Vendome to be built on the plot of land where her house once stood. Jones, a miner who struck it rich, wanted to build a fine, dignified hotel suitable for his sweetheart. But when his lady scorned him shortly after completion of the building, he changed his mind and turned it into a boarding house for miners. In time, the boarding house assumed its intended role as a hotel, renting rooms on a nightly basis—a single for $1.50 per night and a double for $2.50—advertising itself as "A Place Where Particular People Will Be Satisfied" (according to historian Elizabeth Ruffner). We know from the November 1917 edition of *Yavapai Magazine* that the hotel was the answer to one of the town's dire needs—lodging: "Hotel Vendome's construction will fill a need for housing in the town which is crucial even when the summer visitors are induced to return home." It also conceivably provided temporary residences for the families of tuberculosis sufferers who came to Prescott in the 1920s to breathe the clean mountain air and benefit from the restorative climate.

Abby Byr, one of the hotel's most famous ghosts, was one such tuberculosis victim who came to Arizona during this period. Legend has it that arrangements were made for Abby and her husband to be caretakers of the hotel, until they eventually lost their positions (due to an unspecified financial hardship or tax dispute). The new owners negotiated to allow Abby, her husband and her cat, Nobel, to remain in the hotel free of charge, which they did, or at least they did until Abby's husband deserted her. Not long after she was abandoned in 1921, both she and her cat died in their "complimentary" room, Room 16.

During the 1930s, the Vendome was a home-away-from-home for many movie cowboys filming Westerns in the area. Silent Western movie star Tom Mix, for example, rented a room for a year at a time. It's been passed down through generations of owners that the actor preferred to stay in the area known today as Room 3, which then extended to the space where the office is now located. The room's closet has a mysterious stairway that climbs up to the ceiling and stops. Before the opening was sealed with drywall, the stairs would have led into Room 17.

Renovations on the hotel began in 1983, although the interior and exterior of Hotel Vendome are essentially unchanged. Many continue to enjoy the whimsical Western/Victorian atmosphere within its walls. As you walk into the old lobby, there is a sense of being transported back in time to the Prescott of the early 1900s, and this feeling of utter timelessness prevails throughout the hotel. The wide verandas spanning across both levels of the building hearken back to simpler days and leave you wanting to just sit in one of the rocking chairs and watch the world pass by. Kathie and Frank Langford, Hotel Vendome's newest owners/innkeepers, have stayed true to the hotel's history and character, making it the kind of place you want to visit for a spell.

Ghosts

The most famous ghost story connected with this hotel is about Abby Byr and her faithful cat, Nobel. The story, related to me by Kathie, goes that in 1921, Abby (who suffered from severe tuberculosis) sent her husband out one day for more medication. For long hours, she waited and waited. But her husband never returned. It's said that Abby took to her bed, waiting and despairing, refusing to eat or drink. She reportedly died of starvation, dehydration and loneliness—loneliness for human contact—but her cat never deserted her. Her faithful cat, Nobel, stayed by her side until he, too, died of starvation. Abby's ghost and that of her cat began to appear in the hotel shortly after World War II.

Many guests have had Abby encounters in Room 16. Her ghost is believed to be responsible for the ghostly happenings in the room. The TV, lights and ceiling fans turn on and off by themselves. In the bathroom, the faucets turn themselves on as well, and puddles of water mysteriously appear. The doorknobs rattle at will, and the "Do Not Disturb" sign has been seen spinning around the handle. (Perhaps Abby's ghost has a problem with remaining "undisturbed" for too long.)

Room 16 is also a place of bizarre sensory experiences. Guests have heard what sounds like a cat scratching from inside the closet and have been awakened by the sound of a cat purring or meowing loudly. The smell of strong floral perfume sometimes lingers in the air, and guests' belongings have been moved (and not by housekeeping!). Personal items wind up outside of suitcases, scattered nearby, in a way that suggests feline play. Another gentleman reported that something raised his feet six inches off the bed!

One recent guest placed the stuffed white decorative cat found in the room (one of the items left as a gift for Abby and present, among other things, when the Langfords bought the hotel, these mementos are a part of the room's furnishings) from the bed to the seat of a nearby chair. In the morning, the cat was found in a curled-up position on the floor. This guest also felt something—person or cat—sitting on the bed with him that morning.

MVD Ghostchaser team members Chris and Shiela McCurdy took the "Abby challenge" one Saturday night. Shiela was in the bathroom taking a shower when she began to hear loud meowing coming from the other room. She came out of the shower to find her husband asleep and heard more meowing coming from the closet. When she opened the door, she found nothing.

Ghost encounters are not limited to Room 16, however. Guests in Room 10 said someone passed *through* their door at about 4:00 a.m. Another man walking through the first floor hallway noticed that his shadow was not in sync with his body movements. He stopped, but the shadow continued on!

Bent on thoroughly investigating the hotel for ourselves, the MVD Ghostchasers recently booked every room in Hotel Vendome for a ghost-hunting extravaganza. We were able to videotape an investigation that swept the hotel from top to bottom. Forty ghost hunters broke up into five teams and used various ghost-hunting tools and techniques in a mass effort to detect the presence of Abby and Nobel.

Team One held a mock tea party in the lobby, hoping Abby would opt to join them since spirits like to interact. Even though they formally went upstairs and invited her down to the lobby for the tea, she did not choose to grace them with her company. Photos, meters and other recording devices did not pick up on her presence.

Team Two investigated the grounds behind the hotel using dowsing rods to locate a cat rumored to be buried there. They were able to find three pet graves, one of which just might belong to Nobel.

Team Three gathered in front of Room 16 with an array of cat toys: balls on string, jingling objects, play mice and other things. They were using a thermal scanner and EMF meters to detect Nobel's presence, hoping to entice him into "playing" by moving the toys. Although the readings did not fluctuate noticeably, they felt Nobel become skittish and dart from Room 16 across the hall into Room 17. (We all found it intriguing that the guest who was staying in Room 17 was allergic to cats and suffered an allergy attack as soon as

Nobel's ghost arrived.)

Team Four covered the downstairs hallway, seeking the shadowy figure seen moving along the wall. They used a night vision camera and various energy meters. They found no evidence of the presence that night.

Team Five conducted a seance in Room 16 to see if Abby had any messages to deliver. The channelers sensed that Abby wanted all of us to know she means no harm to anyone, especially guests, and she does not want anyone to be afraid to sleep in her room.

Two of the ghost hunters present spent the night in Room 16. These ladies reported feeling the presence of a cat in bed with them. They could also hear purring, and one of them reported that something flicked one of her earrings. Inside the bathroom, the little shampoo and lotion bottles were knocked over as if something had been playing with them. It seems that Nobel paid them a visit!

If you wake up in the middle of the night and see flashes of bright lights or hear a sudden loud noise—perhaps even the sound of someone running up and down the stairs—it just might be Abby Byr and her faithful, playful cat, Nobel.

Address: 230 South Cortez Street, Prescott, AZ 86303
Phone: 928-776-0900; Toll Free: 888-468-3583
Fax: 928-771-0395
Email: vendomehotel@aol.com
Website: www.vendomehotel.com
Contact: Frank and Kathie Langford, owners
Lodging: 21 guest rooms with large, tiled, private baths offering shower/tub combinations and pull-chain toilets
Amenities: cable TV, phone, AC, complimentary continental breakfast, oak furnishings, original woodwork, handmade patchwork quilts

Buford House Bed & Breakfast
Tombstone

History

Listed on the National Register of Historic Places, the Buford House was designed and built in 1880 by George Buford, a mine owner and mining engineer originally from East Texas, one year before the famous Gunfight at the OK Corral occurred. Buford built the two-story adobe house during the height of the Tombstone silver mining bonanza and brought a little bit of European flavor and class to the wild town with his home, even installing two sunken, tiled concrete bathtubs on the ground floor. Today, the Garden Room features one of the old sunken tubs.

The house was once the home of George Daves Jr., whose father, George Daves Sr., lodged in the house after Buford. The young Daves was twenty-one years old and in love with Petra Edmonds, the seventeen-year-old across the street. They had known each other during the five years since his family moved to Tombstone. Petra had befriended George, and over time, their friendship turned to love. George wished to make her his bride but before he proposed, he wanted to have an honest amount of money, enough to provide her with a comfortable home and financial security. So he left Tombstone for the silver mines located forty-five minutes away from Casa Grande. For nine months he toiled in the mines, enduring many backbreaking hardships. When George returned, prepared to propose, he discovered that Petra had turned her attentions toward another young man. He was heartbroken—his dreams shattered—and his heartache soon turned into rage.

On April 14, 1888, George loaded a gun and walked across the street to Petra's house. As she ran from him, heading for her front porch, George fired the gun four times, hitting her twice and severely wounding her. The first bullet entered the top of her right shoulder—resulting in a rather minor flesh wound—but the other bullet entered her back, just to the right of the lowest point of her shoulder blade, passing through the right lung and coming out on the left of her right armpit. Horrified and grief-stricken, assuming her injuries were fatal, George then turned the gun on himself, pointed it to his right temple and took his own life. He died almost instantly. However, in a miraculous and ironic twist of fate, Petra's wounds turned out not to be fatal. A doctor by the name of Goodfellow attended her wounds and was able to remove the bullet and save Petra from death. She lived another 50 years without her star-crossed lover.

(The preceding information was condensed from an article written by Douglas D. Martin, published April 14, 1888, in *The Tombstone Epitaph*.)

Over the years, George's old house has been home to some of Tombstone's most prominent citizens, including two sheriffs, a mayor, a marshal and a state senator. And no, the Earps never owned the property. Brenda Reger opened the Buford House as a Bed and Breakfast in 1990. In 1999, Richard and Ruth Allen purchased the Buford House and have been making improvements ever since.

The Allens like their guests to feel special (including the guest who prefers to hang around unseen) and so carry on the tradition of providing a hearty, homestyle country breakfast each morning. There is a territorial-style wraparound porch where guests can relax to that slower pace that Tombstone seems to emit. The Buford House Bed and Breakfast's laid-back atmosphere is enhanced by the goldfish in the pond, the gardens and the birds that flock to the feeders. Coming here is like visiting Grandma's house in the country (except Grandma's house probably doesn't have ghosts!).

Ghosts

Richard and Ruth Allen learned they had at least one permanent guest at the Buford soon after their purchase. It seems that George has remained within the walls of his homestead, and his ghost loves to play pranks on the guests. He shuts off the air conditioning in guest rooms during the middle of the night and has been known to play with the feet of female guests. His casual flirtations with the womenfolk include gently tugging on their ponytails and lightly touching their hair or the back of their heads. Some of the ladies have allegedly felt him kissing them on the back of the neck and running his fingers through their hair.

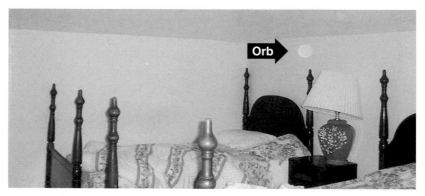

A crooked lampshade in the Nellie Cashman Room
Is this ghost mischief or coincidence?

The Allens report that all of the dogs and cats that reside at Buford House love George. Their watchful eyes often follow the invisible specter around the grounds. George, in turn, seems to love the animals; if they want to go back indoors after romping outside but the Allens seem to have forgotten about them, George will ring the doorbell to remind them to let their pets return inside. (Richard reports that George also rings the doorbell in the wee hours of the morning–say, 3:00 a.m.– just to assure everyone he's home for the night.)

George's apparition has been *seen* on a few rare occasions as well. One holiday when Richard was decorating the family Christmas tree and Ruth was in the kitchen, Ruth glanced up at the tree and saw the wavy, transparent outline of a young man. He was smiling and seemed to be watching Richard as he hung tinsel on the tree. She saw George several more times that day, but these days, the Allens say they "feel" George more than they "see" him.

There is a second, female ghost who also abides in the Buford House. The spirit of this elderly lady is usually seen in the Garden Room where she is believed to have passed away. She is reputed to have hated dark clothing and always wore soft, light colors. This lady in white generally makes her appearance between 3:00 a.m. and 5:00 a.m. and tends to appear to the men in the house.

The spirit has likewise been spotted upstairs in the Wicker Room, slowly rocking back and forth in the chair. A startled guest woke up to find the ghost of the elderly lady in the room with her and asked the spirit if she would please leave. The spirit stayed firm and responded, "This is my room. You need to get out." Although the woman was startled for a few minutes, she did not heed this directive. The spirit faded away, and she was eventually able to get back to sleep.

Who goes there? Orbs hovering in the Wicker Room bedchamber.

Also within the Wicker Room, a strange light often glows. Though it appears to be shining in the window from outside, there are no street lights or other light sources near the house–no lamps, lanterns, porch lights or anything else–that could emit or reflect light. All that can be seen is a bright beam of light that blinks, and we found nothing that could logically explain or account for this phenomenon.

One more ghost lives with the Allens; Richard related that a ghostly pet resides here, too. Several guests have reported feeling a cat rubbing against their legs. Expecting to see a cat, they look down but see nothing–no trace of a kitty in sight.

Richard told me that the ghosts are like part of the family and that they treat them as such. George comes by almost upon request. When they call out his name or ask him to come out, George will often pop in and make an appearance by moving something. The Allens enjoy sharing their house with spirits and sharing the spirits in their house with guests.

Address: 113 Safford Street, P.O. Box 98, Tombstone, AZ 85638
Phone: 520-457-3969
Email: Bufordhousebandb@aol.com
Contact: Richard and Ruth Allen, owners
Lodging: 5 rooms
Amenities: 2 rooms with private bath and 3 with shared, sinks in rooms, TV in common room, full country breakfast

Larian Motel
Tombstone

History

The Larian Motel was built in 1957 to accommodate the town's growing tourist industry. It is situated along a stretch of Highway 80 that runs through Tombstone. Located at the core of Tombstone's renowned historic district, the motel was built on land that once had high-energy businesses on it: a gun shop, general store and a Chinese shop. Objects that allude to the site's history have been unearthed in the motel's back lot: Chinese artifacts, spent bullet casings, and old-time bottles and horseshoes, among other things.

Constructed in a horseshoe formation, the Larian is ideally situated for those with a desire to explore the town. Just paces away are famous historic attractions, including the OK Corral, Crystal Palace Saloon, Big Nose Kate's Saloon, the Tombstone Court House and the Bird Cage Theatre.

Larian Motel owner and operator Gordon Anderson has been running this operation since September 1980. Having lived in Tombstone for over twenty years, he has acquired a vast knowledge of the town's history. Gordon is also a well-known local actor who has performed on the stage as well as prime time; he played a ghost in a scene of an *A & E Haunted*

History episode that featured "The Town Too Tough To Die." Perhaps that's why spirits feel so comfortable checking in at the Larian.

Ghosts

Gordon Anderson led team member Mark Christoph and me on a brief tour of the premises. The energies of the past have carried through into this building (relatively new in the scheme of Tombstone's timeline). Most of the ghost activity occurs on the motel's west side.

Gordon told us that he and his mother have both heard mysterious music in the vicinity of the motel. He described the experience as strange and hard to explain, but added that the music does not last for long.

Due to her psychic abilities, Catrina, a former housekeeper, claimed to have had many ghostly experiences as she cleaned. She reported sensing a friendly presence, most often within the original area of the motel, in Rooms 1, 2, 3 and 4.

Entering Room 1, we felt a comfortable, peaceful, friendly spirit atmosphere. While we could feel someone watching us as we investigated, it was still a very welcoming room, as if the spirits in there liked us.

Jean Mosher of Green Valley, Arizona, shared the following story about an experience that she and her twin, Joanie Talley of Southern California, had during a recent visit:

My twin and I have had numerous telepathy and other sorts of ESP experiences throughout our 71 years and accept that we are a part of each other. It was the 7th of February, 2004, and my sister Joanie and I had reserved a room at the Larian Motel. (We had stayed there once before in a room across the way.) We had so enjoyed the town and townspeople and had spent a good amount of time in Big Nose Kate's Saloon, taking pictures and talking to a few of the cowboys, one of whom had twins in his family as well. Neither one of us drink at all, however, so we were of clear mind and sober thought when we returned. This night we were in Room 3, the Doc Holliday Room.

Returning to our room around 10:00 p.m., my twin

and I readied for bed, watched a little TV and turned out the lights at about 11:00 p.m., falling right to sleep. At 12:30 a.m., I woke with a start, feeling as if there was someone in the room with us. I looked over at Joanie's bed and saw that she was still sleeping. I sat up and looked around the room but saw nothing, so I lay back down but with an unsettled feeling. I still felt someone else was in the room, but I had looked around and bolted the door as soon as we were inside. Finally, I was able to fall asleep and slept fitfully till morning.

We awoke on Sunday, the 8th, and nothing was mentioned by either of us. We got ready, packed the car and went to the Longhorn Restaurant for breakfast. While waiting for our order, Joanie said to me, 'The funniest thing happened last night.' I asked her what it was. She said that she woke up at about 12:30 a.m. and had a feeling someone was in the room with us. She sat up and looked around but saw nothing. After laying back down, she finally got up to use the powder room and went back to bed thinking it had been me that was up and around, and she went back to sleep.

Can you imagine my shock when she told me this story as I had lived it the night before? She asked me what was wrong, so I told her of my same experience. The main difference between our ghost encounters was our responses to it: I felt it was a friendly ghost, but Joanie related that she said a prayer for God's protection when she lay back down.

We were both stunned, and yet the only real surprise was the part about how the ghost had affected us differently. We laughed and wondered if it had indeed been Doc Holliday paying us a visit.

Now that's spooky!

Room 3 has a reputation for being a "lost and found" area, where guests' personal items turn up missing but somehow return later. One gentleman's experience as a guest here serves as a good example of this phenomenon. He had set his glasses down on a table only to discover several minutes later that they had, by some unknown means, disappeared. He searched everywhere in the room for the spectacles, even calling in housekeeping to help him search. Later that day, after a day of Tombstone sightseeing, the man returned to his room to find his glasses in the same location where he had placed them earlier!

Room 4 is the Wyatt Earp Room. Mark (who is highly intuitive) felt the presence of a large, elderly, white-haired "man" when we first entered the room who he was able to see in his mind's eye. Mark said that the man was wearing a white shirt and, from the style of his shirt and trousers, he seemed to be a time traveler from the 1950s or 60s–likely a man who had visited the Larian while he was on vacation. The friendly man watched us for a few minutes before his energies faded away. He had been standing near the bed until he vanished.

If you come down to Tombstone's Larian Motel, be sure to loosen your stays or put on your Stetson, and it wouldn't hurt to practice your moseying. Bedding down at the Larian will take you away to the days of gunfights and the OK Corral. Spending a night here could also acquaint you with some of Tombstone's old-time visitors, from wranglers and gunslingers to black market hustlers and retro tourists.

Address: Highway 80, P.O. Box 224, Tombstone, AZ
              85638
Phone: 520-457-2272
Fax: 520-457-2272
Email: larianmotel@theriver.com
Website: www.tombstonemotels.com
Contact: Gordon Anderson, owner
Lodging: 14 rooms
Amenities: large rooms, all ground level, in-room coffee,
              cable TV, king and queen sized beds, within
              walking distance of historic Allen Street

H--t-l --n-jr-s

Tucson

History

The Hotel Congress takes up an entire triangular city block in downtown Tucson. Built in 1919 during the height of train travel, the brick and marble hotel served the Southern Pacific Railroad passengers who arrived and departed from the train station across the street. Local residents came to the establishment to frolic in the Tap Room. It was the perfect hangout for the flapper era of the "Roaring Twenties," where the younger members of this generation would breeze in to enjoy a night of drinking and dancing.

Although the true tale of their capture has become shrouded in years of embellishment—a part of local mythology—it has been determined that two members of John Dillinger's gang checked into the Hotel Congress on January 21, 1934. It is likely that Charlie Makley, Russell Clark and Clark's girlfriend, Opal Long, were keeping a low profile here following a spree of bank robberies in the Midwest. It is not known if Dillinger himself was a guest here at this time. However it may be, early in the morning of January 23, an oil furnace in the basement near the elevator shaft caught fire, and the flames rapidly shot up the elevator shaft to the then-existing third floor, alerting the notorious guests staying there. Preparing to rush from their rooms to the street, the members of the Dillinger Gang took so long getting their luggage together that when they were finally ready to escape, they found that the smoke and flames had trapped them in the burning building. Firemen quickly swung a ladder to the window ledge, and with the aid of the Tucson Fire Department, the two men and one woman descended the ladder to the street. At the urgent request of the gang members, along with a $50 tip, two firemen went back up to the third floor to rescue the heavy baggage from their rooms.

Just days after this fire completely destroyed the third floor, the firemen who had unknowingly assisted Dillinger's crew were flipping through pages of *True Detective* when they suddenly recognized the men who had tipped them to rescue their luggage. The police were quickly notified, leading to the capture of Dillinger and three members of his notorious gang on January 25th: Harry Pierpont, Russell Clark and Charlie Makley. The suspiciously heavy luggage that the firemen had retrieved (described in the *Arizona Daily Star* as "some of the smartest seen here,"quite a tip-off of its own in those days), contained machine guns, pistols, ammunition, bullet-proof vests and $23,816 in stolen bills.

The fire-gutted third floor was never restored, so Hotel Congress instead became a two-story establishment with forty rooms on the second floor. Much of the original furniture has been maintained, featuring iron beds and black and white tiled bathrooms connected to rooms with vintage appeal. Within the lobby, you'll find a 1920s-1930s Art Deco design with a painted Native American motif in bold colors. There are even old wooden phone booths with glass windows and one of the hotel's original safes, as well as old photos of the hotel and Tucson.

The Tap Room has become a laid back bar since the days of prohibition, and Club Congress is a popular live music venue that attracts many. The café (which doubles as a coffee shop) offers eclectic fare, running the gamut from Indian, Japanese and Thai to Mexican, Mediterranean and old-fashioned American cuisine. It attracts a clientele of both local and international visitors with its Southwestern charm. It also attracts guests from the other side.

Ghosts

The MVD Ghostchasers did a walk-through investigation of Hotel Congress on a Saturday evening. I reported our arrival to the front desk clerk, Myrna, who called someone on the phone to announce in a manner straight out of *Poltergeist*, "They're heeere!" I took a great picture of two huge orbs greeting us on the staircase right away. It seemed that the spirits were checking us out before we went upstairs.

Going up or coming down?

Myrna gave us the keys to one of the few rooms unoccupied on a Saturday night, Room 210, a rather modest space that still caters to simple 1930s and 1940s needs: no TV, just radio. The bathroom was on the small side, and while investigating it, team member Stu Sobrane became trapped in the shower stall! I think we attracted the spirits with our laughter as we poured back out into the hall.

Loretta, our guide, met us in the hallway. She pointed out the area of the hall where many of the housekeeping staff have seen a man in a seersucker suit walking from room to room–entering and exiting without opening a door.

Next she led us down to Room 242. There had been one notorious suicide in the room many years ago. Many guests hear disembodied voices and crying. Some have reported the sensation of being touched by an invisible hand while in here.

At the conclusion of the tour, she left us to do more exploring on our own. Many of us ventured up to what had once been the third floor–now the roof of the hotel. The rooftop had a wonderful view of the city of Tucson. As we wandered about, we took several more photos on top of this "phantom floor" and in the hallways. Again, many orbs appeared on our digital cameras, and the activity seemed to be strongest on the east side of the building, the same area where the female apparition has been sighted.

The hotel has that speakeasy kind of feeling to it. Perhaps the spirits present were enjoying the jazz band playing in the lobby below.

Address:	311 East Congress Street, Tucson, AZ 85701
Phone:	520-622-8848; Toll Free: 800-722-8848
Fax:	520-792-6366
Email:	reservations@hotelcongress.com
Website:	www.hotelcongress.com
Contact:	David Slutes, manager
Lodging:	40 rooms
Amenities:	rooms have baths, phones and radios, bar, pub and café within walking distance of other local clubs and restaurants

Santa Rita Hotel
Tucson

History

Located near the entrance of Tucson's historic El Presidio district in the neighborhood known as Armory Park, the Santa Rita Hotel was built in downtown Tucson during 1904. It stands upon the former site of Camp Tucson—a temporary U.S. Army camp which was renamed Camp Lowell in 1866 (created to reestablish "law and order" after the Civil War). Its bricks were made nearby at an old kiln that was recently unearthed by a Tucson geological group (the kiln's foundation was discovered just a few blocks away on Congress Street). The Tucson Pressed Brick Company (1894-1963) provided the material for the Santa Rita Hotel, St. Augustine Cathedral, Rincon High School and many other local buildings.

In 1904, over two thousand Tucsonians celebrated the hotel's grand opening, coming out to view its roof garden, dance hall and modern technology. It was constructed to fulfill Tucson's need for a luxury resort hotel and was considered very posh due to its modern plumbing, bathrooms, electricity and phones. The Santa Rita was also the first Arizona hotel to have an up-and-running elevator. Renovated in 1998, this boutique-style hotel continues to be a desert oasis with a unique Mexican ambiance.

This historic hotel remains one of the only hotels in Arizona to have received the honored Choice Hotels International Gold Award for outstanding service. In addition to such hospitality, there are plenty of things here to please the senses, especially the eye and palate: marble floors in the lobby, a sunken lounge area with pleasantly overstuffed furniture, the outdoors waterfall (one of the delightful remnants of the original hotel), and folk art upon the walls of Café Poca Cosa, a dynamite Mexican restaurant. And don't forget about all the ghosts!

Ghosts

One of the oldest hotels in Tucson, the Santa Rita Hotel has a vast collection of spirits in its rooms and hallways. The MVD Ghostchasers were fortunate to receive a private tour of the facility led by Trish Kleismit, one of the former coordinators of the hotel. Trish gave us some history of the building and pointed out the original artwork and furniture still in the lobby. Hopping into the elevator, we headed for the eighth floor and were escorted down a hallway to the loft rooms, considered the most spirit active in the hotel.

Room 813 is the site where a woman was murdered. The victim was allegedly strangled in the bedroom doorway. Although the details of the crime are unclear, her presence is often felt in this area. Regardless of the how or why, there is a cold chill and feeling of desolation that permeates the atmosphere in the room.

A couple staying in the other loft room next door, Room 815, thought they saw a figure standing behind the curtains. Somewhat unnerved by the optical illusion, they went upstairs to bed. In the middle of the night, the gentleman headed down to the kitchen to make himself a cup of tea. After a few soothing sips, he placed the cup on the table, returned upstairs and fell back asleep. The following morning, after the couple made their way downstairs, they sat down to breakfast and found fresh red lipstick prints on the cold cup of tea.

During our investigation of Room 815, team member Maureen Mustaca and I both saw what looked like a body standing behind these same drapes. At first glance, the curtains bulged outward like someone was wrapped inside them. There was no one else visibly present (we checked!), but we felt like someone was watching us the entire time we were inside the room.

Room 822 is an exceptional haunted area for several reasons. The first reason has to do with the room's location and physical history. A more compelling reason has to do with the tragedy that occurred here. The third, and most pertinent, reason has to do with what has happened to a member of the Arizona Opera Company when he stays in the room.

First off, a portion of the room occupies what was once the old manual elevator shaft (the bedroom encompasses the closed-off shaft itself). Since thunderstorms produce magnetic and electrical energy that attracts ghosts to paranormally active areas, it is not surprising that the room contains increased levels of ghost activity during these storms. The turret that stands on the roof above the room has even been struck by lightning (the ghosts must have piled in following that event!).

Rumored to be the home of resident ghost John Ferguson, Room 822 possesses a sinister reputation to go with its reputed tragic past. This is the room where Ferguson is believed to have been involved in a murder/suicide. Team member Becky Strong relayed the following information and her personal experience regarding the Ferguson story:

The story goes that an obsessive-compulsive man by the name of John Ferguson, believed to have been a butler, at one time lived in Room 822. His wife had an affair and ended up pregnant. John killed her in a jealous rage and felt so guilty about it that he hung himself in what was then the elevator shaft. When the hotel was remodeled in the 1980s, the elevators were moved to a different location inside the hotel, and the elevator shaft where John hung himself was turned into the bedroom of Room 822. John, a deeply religious man, will not pass to the other side because he believes he will go to hell as punishment for committing suicide. He is quite up-to-date on current events and loves to participate in ghost investigations. Through psychics, he asks what certain equipment is for, how it works and so on. He also hates messes, so if you leave a closet or drawer opened, he tidies it up. He also turns the lights and television set on or off while you are away. He straightens beds as well.

My husband and I stayed in Room 822 and had an experience there, but I am not quite sure that our ghost was Ferguson. The hotel did not have eight stories until renovations in the 1980s, so Ferguson would have had to commit his murder/suicide after the 1980s when an eighth floor was created.

The rumors imply that the tragedy occurred in the 1930s or 1940s, but there is no research to verify that claim.

Through my research at the Arizona Historical Society, the hotel housed low income residents in the 1970s, until the renovations in the 1980s made it a high class hotel once more, only this time, with eight floors.

Perhaps the murder/suicide occurred in the 1980s, or maybe the room's hauntings are not the work of John Ferguson after all!

There are the ghost accounts from the opera man to consider. We spoke to a gentleman from the Arizona Opera Company who has adopted Room 822 as his own whenever he is in town because he enjoys the room's spirit energy and the ghost phenomena that tend to occur when he stays here. He stated that the lights, electricity and TV turn themselves on and off and he told us a story about how the bathroom door kept closing on its own during one of his visits (he wanted it open so the bathroom was easily accessible in the dark). He kept opening the door. The door kept closing. It went on like this throughout the night. He also reported that tiles in the bathroom ceiling began to vibrate. When we tested the door, we found that it was balanced and functioning properly. An outside force would have to shut it since it doesn't swing closed by itself.

This gentleman described other fantastic experiences he

had during the same visit. The curtains in the living room began to blow into the air, about two feet straight out from the window! The air conditioner was not on at the time, and the windows are sealed. Again, we tested the effect that having the air on would have. The curtains still did not blow.

A friend who was visiting as his guest stayed in the room only one time. In the course of his stay, he saw an older "woman" floating above him while he was in bed. The spirit appeared to be an elderly lady, and she hovered above him in the old elevator shaft area. She then dived down and swooshed across the room, where she vanished. (That might deter a person from another visit!)

While we were investigating the top floor, our EMF meters jumped to the red zone in the hallway outside the suite where psychics have felt a presence. Using a digital camera, we photographed orbs on the ceiling of the bedroom near the sealed-off elevator shaft.

Next stop was a visit to the fourth floor. (We had to be very quiet as this is where airline crews rest between flights.) At the end of the hall, there had been a nursery for the children of hotel employees. We learned that there was a very tragic fire on this level in the 1940s in which many children died. We captured one lone orb in the hallway.

We moved back up to the sixth floor in search of the pint-sized ghosts that have been something of a nuisance to some guests, as well as a source of bafflement. One guest reported being constantly disturbed by the sounds of children running up and down the hallway. When he opened the door to silence them, he saw the group round a corner that led to a dead end. He kept watching and waiting for them to return. They did not. It seems that they disappeared into another time.

As we proceeded down the hall, team member Gary Tone and I suddenly came across a cold spot. Cold energy shot through our bodies. When former team member Kathy Pepera joined us, we began to play a ghostly game of Red Rover with the unseen children. Strange as it may seem, we held hands and started to call out individual names. Each time we could feel cold energies running past our linked arms.

I remember calling Johnny (cold chill), Susan (cold chill) and Mary (more cold chill). We played the last few rounds by calling, "Send all the kids over!" and felt a major cold rush pass through us. We all felt these cold sensations. In the photographs we took, five or six energy orbs appear in formation as the children's ghosts played the game with us.

Trish then took us downstairs to an old, unused kitchen. It was here that a chef and his kitchen staff were savagely murdered years ago as they prepared a meal. In spite of the gruesome history, we did not feel any presence here.

She then took us into a dark hallway on the ground floor where voices and crying are often heard. We all stood very quietly, listening. Nothing unusual happened, however, and the EMF meters showed no variance in readings.

Specific ghosts regularly haunt other areas of the Santa Rita as well. Outside in the pool area is the spirit of a young toddler who drowned. The story passed down by hotel staff says that the toddler was searching for his mother when he fell into the water. Many poolside guests have reported hearing a belly flop and splashing water accompanied by a baby crying.

A little boy spirit haunts the elevator. He is rumored to have been the son of a "working girl." A bellboy watched over the child as his mother plied her trade within the hotel. Apparently, the child still plays in the elevator.

One evening, a hotel clerk heard the sound of high heels clicking on the tile floor near the large pillars. In fact, she saw a shadowy figure moving from pillar to pillar. A psychic later advised her, "Don't worry about the lady. She is just going to work." This psychic felt that the shadow belonged to the spirit of the prostitute whose son played (and continues to play) in the elevator while she was working.

In the lounge area, a gentleman guest was walking underneath a light when it turned itself on and off several times. It turns out that a woman was once beaten and robbed in this area. Her spirit evidently has some sort of vendetta because she only pulls pranks like this on men.

Trish informed us there are secret crawlspace passageways sealed off under every other floor that have never been explored. Showing us a set of blueprints from the hotel's archives, she explained that the tunnels had been sealed during renovations. She believed that items from the hotel's past were "entombed" within them, and she told us about the antique furniture that was gathered and buried underground when they tore down the old ballroom to expand the hotel's parking lot facilities.

There are many spirits caught in time within the walls of the Santa Rita. And even though there is no longer a valet service at the Santa Rita Hotel, many guests still see attendants from the past manning the booths at the entrances. Some have even met phantom valets who park their cars. They seem so real, until they vanish.

Address: 88 East Broadway Blvd., Tucson, AZ 85701
Phone: 520-622-4000; Toll Free: 800-CLARION
Fax: 520-620-0376
Email: dosazar@aol.com
Website: www.choicehotels.com
Contact: Susan Azar, director of sales
Lodging: 139 rooms and 22 suites, including 2 presiden-
             tial suites, 6 two-story lofts and 23 executive
             suites
Amenities: complimentary breakfast buffet, restaurant,
             hair dryer, in-room coffee, refrigerator, micro-
             wave, iron, data port phones with dial-up
             Internet access, cable TV, outdoor pool, hot tub,
             sauna, waterfall, library, gym, laundry service
             and dry cleaning, a small deposit for approved
             animal guests

Red Garter
Bed & Bakery
Williams

History

August Tetzlaff was a German tailor who built this two-story building during 1897 in downtown Williams' Saloon Row. (The original keystone with Tetzlaff's name and the building's construction date stamped on it is still above the arched entrance.) Tetzlaff meant for his establishment to satisfy the needs of cowboys, loggers and railroad workers who had settled near the frontier town; the building housed a saloon on the first floor and a bordello upstairs, where the ladies of the night often dangled out of windows, offering lewd invitations, as well as other "come hither" looks and maneuvers, in an attempt to lure passers-by inside. There was a private entrance on the building's side that led to a steep flight of steps nicknamed the "Cowboy's Endurance Test" and on up to the "soiled doves." In later years, tourists heading to the Grand Canyon by railway and, later still, those who stopped off here from Route 66 would stop and spend the night in the vacant rooms.

Longino Mora operated the saloon for many years, bootlegging liquor out the back door during Prohibition years. Mora, a pioneer born in 1848 at the end of the Mexican-American War, is a prominent figure in Williams' history. After working for the U.S. Cavalry, hauling freight to army posts across vast stretches of desert, he was a scout who chased Geronimo and Cochise throughout Mexico and the Arizona Territory. During his travels, he passed through the Williams area before the town existed, once waiting on "High School Hill" for a traveling band of Indians to move on so he could water his animals. Known also for being a "good" Catholic, Mora was married five times and fathered twenty-five children. (All of his wives were from Old Mexico; two died of cholera and two died in childbirth. His last wife, Clara, was fifty years his junior and bore his last child when he was eighty.) He was apparently something of a regional celebrity as well. Guests such as Arizona Governor George W. P. Hunt would come to visit Mora and his large family at the saloon.

In preparation for statehood, the government of the Arizona Territory banned prostitution and gambling in 1907. The law was loosely enforced by Arizona Rangers, but many towns were essentially self-governing, and they mostly chose to ignore the illegal status of these profitable enterprises, especially since many a town's economy depended on the trade. Local ordinances were passed to regulate where and when brothels could operate. The constable, hired to enforce these ordinances, collected his wages from the girls themselves. As a result, the saloon and bordello business in Williams continued to flourish until the mid-1940s.

Around this time, a tragic murder was committed on the steps of the Red Garter. A prostitute stabbed her customer in the back, causing him to fall down the stairs and through the front door where he died on the street. The fallout from these kinds of incidents are what finally caused a major crackdown on bordellos and the saloons that acted as a front for them.

The final blow came when many of the area's potential customers were called to WW II.

A colorful storyteller and historian, John Holst has his fingers on the pulse of his Bed and Bakery's less-than-virtuous past, which has, at various points, also been a Chinese restaurant, opium den, general store and boarding house. The Red Garter Bed & Bakery is a part of the notable Saloon Row business district listed on the National Register of Historic Places for its Victorian Romanesque architecture. John can explain the connection between the add-ons in the back of the building, the construction of the railroad and the opium trade as he regales you with one of his enthralling stories. Incidentally, from 1901 until the late 1930s, the saloon also boasted a two-story outhouse in the back that was built after the town's big fire. (John shares that the second floor "facilities" were apparently located to the side of the downstairs privy. The building was eventually torn down after indoors plumbing was installed.)

John Holst bought the boarded-up building in 1979 and returned it to usable condition. It was converted into a BBQ restaurant in 1984. Ten years later, he began to run the establishment himself, transforming the eight former brothel rooms into four expansive guest rooms with a Western Victorian flavor and switching the downstairs from restaurant to bakery. Guests face temptation of a different sort these days: a variety of enticing pastry treats from the bakery!

Ghosts

Downstairs in the bakery, owner and innkeeper John Holst was eager to show team member Megan Taylor and me a picture taken in the Red Garter Saloon during the Depression. Although the bar and poker tables are craftily hidden behind a divider (it was taken during the Prohibition Era), clearly visible in the photo are Longino Mora with his fifth wife Clara, his twenty-fifth child Carmina and some members of his staff. There is also a mysterious lady standing behind the counter. In the photo, the petite Mexican woman is standing in front of a mirror, but there is an anomaly—the mirror does not reflect her image! Megan photographed ectoplasm in the area where the unreflected woman had been standing. Our EMF meters picked up high readings in this area, where the counter once was.

Moving upstairs with John, we began to investigate the rooms. Most paranormal activity seems to take place in Room 1, known as the Best Gal's Room (this is the room with windows that overlook the street below). As we approached, Megan and I photographed a few orbs in the upstairs hallway. We immediately found that all the rooms have double locks, and once locked, there is no way that the door can be opened again from the outside. Nevertheless, guests staying in this room have come downstairs, concerned that someone—perhaps a maid or guest—entered their room during the middle of the night.

These mystified guests have reported seeing the spirit of an obviously distressed woman in Room 1. Her hands are typically clutched in front of her, as if she is holding a pillbox, and she has a distraught, sad look on her face. She has been described as a young Hispanic woman with long dark hair in a white nightgown who paces the floor near the foot of the bed and vanishes. A guest who claims to have made contact with this spirit says her name is Eva, or Eve.

In another room, it seems some of the working girls have come back to ply their trade. Unsuspecting visitors get quite a shock from these visits. (Most reports come from women, although you would think "the girls" would rather engage male guests; perhaps the men just aren't telling). Female guests have complained of something bouncing on the mattress, and have felt depressions appear on top of it—as if someone was sitting at the foot of the bed. One guest divulged that she woke up to someone stroking her arm. But when she opened her eyes, no one was there. It is not unusual for guests to hear doors slamming and footsteps in the hall and on the staircase, too.

In the years that John has lived upstairs in the hotel, he has become aware of a recurrent oddity. Since he renovated the entire hotel, he has come to know its every creak and rustle. On many nights around 11:30 p.m., he hears a loud "clunk"—what he describes as "a heavy door being shut firmly."

When he first started noticing this aberrant noise, he would get out of bed and go downstairs to check the doors. Wouldn't you know, he found all of them locked—every time. Although he claims to be a skeptic, he fully acknowledges that this is not normal hotel noise.

Perhaps that clunking noise, along with the footsteps people often hear, is just another cowboy coming up to visit his favorite lady?

Address: 137 West Railroad Avenue, Williams, AZ
             86046
Phone: 928-635-1484; Toll Free: 800-328-1484
Email: john@redgarter.com
Website: www.redgarter.com
Contact: John W. Holst, owner
Lodging: 4 rooms with private baths
Amenities: TV, homemade bakery desserts, continental-
             plus breakfast

Yuma

History

The Hotel Lee received its name because it was built on the historic Lee Highway named after General Robert E. Lee. It was built in 1917 on the site where a beautiful adobe house belonging to Virginia Zabala once stood. Virginia loved her adobe's location because it was close to Yuma's only church, the Immaculate Conception. Behind the church was Yuma's only cemetery.

In 1916, the levy broke at the Colorado and Gila River confluence, and the water rushed down Main Street, demolishing almost everything in its path. The beautiful Zabala home was one of the first structures to be destroyed. When the levy broke, the cemetery was also washed away in the flood, and it is estimated that half of the 500 to 700 bodies buried in the cemetery were uprooted from their graves and sent floating down Main Street (the bodies were later re-buried in Potters Field in the now-existing Yuma Cemetery).

The grandson of Virginia Zabala has said his grandmother never recovered from losing the dream home that she had worked so hard to obtain; she continued to dream about the home until the moment she died. Because of this, Virginia Zabala is almost certainly one of the spirits frequenting the Hotel Lee.

One of the first owners of the Hotel Lee was an Italian woman named Mary Darcy (a Darcy by marriage) who bought the hotel in 1922. The layers of lore surrounding this woman paint her as quite the enigmatic figure. By all reports, Mrs. Darcy was a stern woman and very strong-willed. Legend has it that she was proud of the fact that she only shot and killed two people in the hotel. One of these victims was her husband and the other an unsuspecting bill collector who had entered the hotel unannounced.

Mary wanted her hotel to be one of high moral standards (despite the seeming inconsistency in her own moral code). If a couple wanted to stay in the same room, they had to produce their marriage license to get past the registration desk. And regardless of marital status, sexual activity was never permitted on Sunday nights. If she heard two voices coming from a room that, based on registration records, should only have contained one, or if she heard any other "inappropriate" shenanigans happening, patrons were ousted during the middle of the night! It is also said that she would walk the halls at night, holding a glass up to each door and listening for any suspicious noises–noises that did not fit the guest records in her hotel registry.

Mary Darcy also had a mysterious side. On Friday evenings, she and eight of Yuma's other early eccentrics would meet in a back room of the Hotel Lee and hold a séance. It is said that the group practiced black magic and would cast evil spells on those they felt were against them.

Mary Darcy's life is steeped in layers of myth, superstition and gossip. If Mary was a woman who gleefully killed her husband and a man to whom she owed money, then how could she also enforce such Puritan moral standards within these same walls? Was she a religious fanatic in the public sphere and a sinister occultist in private, under cover of night? She seems to have been a woman of many contradictions!

While restoring it to the original European design is an

ongoing effort, the Hotel Lee has recently been converted into a cozy, modernized, air-conditioned Western Victorian hotel with character, spooks and mystery. Owners Bob Glade and Linda Guess purchased the hotel in 2003 and have been upgrading it since then. Added to the National Register of Historic Places in 1984, the building's Mission/Spanish Revival architecture is reason enough to visit. Add the legend of Mary Darcy and the hotel's hauntings to the mix, and you're in for a very interesting visit!

Ghosts

A very spirit-active building, the Hotel Lee is located on a corner of what was once the busy Main Street of Yuma. The Yuma Spirit Hunters, led by Don Swain, have been conducting investigations at the Lee since 1998, when they were called in to investigate strange occurrences and suspected ghost sightings. They have inspected the hotel from top to bottom, setting up equipment overnight, and uncovered much paranormal activity in the process, both on film and other recording devices. (Don has been a tremendous resource to the MVD Ghostchasers as we've investigated this site.)

Don has interacted with several ghosts here, and has recorded phantom voices in the lobby. While packing his ghost-hunting equipment at the end of one night, he left his tape recorder running and proceeded to load equipment into his van. When he played the tape back later, Don discovered that various EVPs had come through, much to his delight. One of his favorites is of a young girl whose voice is mischievous—full of giggles and adventure.

The piano in the lobby has been heard playing music in the middle of the night. And sometimes the lobby clock has stopped, although a ticking sound can still be heard. Guests have smelled the strong odor of chewing tobacco in this area as well, only to find the lone spittoon clean and spotless. Late at night, some have seen shadowy figures darting across the walls and ceilings. There have also been reports of a shadowy reflection in the front lobby window that looked as if it belonged to someone passing by at the top of the staircase. But whoever is casting the shadow can never be found.

Spooky things happen in other places, too. Tools disappear and reappear all through the hotel.

The ghost of an older woman was once sighted walking in the downstairs kitchen area.

In a remote back area of the hotel, there was a spot called the Bible Room, so named because during renovation, a family Bible was recovered and placed on a table in the small room. The room's atmosphere was especially oppressive; Don reported that almost everyone who entered the room felt a sense of despair. Although the room itself no longer exists, many disturbing voices have been heard in this high-energy area. Don has recorded one in particular, a man's low voice, which sounds ghastly and harsh.

Of the approximately fifteen people investigating the hotel–psychics, highly sensitive people and those on my team–we all experienced intensely bad feelings as we took turns entering the room, ranging from stomachaches and headaches to extreme sadness. Some were so powerfully affected by the negativity of the room's atmosphere that they could not walk into it at all.

The MVD Ghostchasers conducted a séance in the workroom directly behind the wall of the front desk (where Mary Darcy is rumored to have sat with her circle of friends many years ago). No major phenomena were recorded on video, but we did photograph some lingering orbs. For some unfathomable reason, children's laughter is sometimes heard emanating from this room.

The spirit of a young girl with dark hair and skin has been spotted carrying towels in the Lee's upstairs hallways. She appears and then suddenly vanishes before your eyes. We believe it is likely that this is the ghost with the mischievous voice–the young girl who was hanging around the lobby as Don packed up equipment.

During the night, you may hear heavy footsteps in the hall. The doors to the rooms sometimes rattle as if someone is checking them. Someone often knocks on the doors during the night as well. For example, Tyler Swain heard knocking at 3:30 a.m. and thought it was his wake-up call for work.

When he opened the door, though, the hall was empty. Many think these creepy events are the work of Mary Darcy as she makes her "after-dark" rounds.

A male ghost who is quite friendly haunts Room 27. He frequently greets guests with a "hello" as they enter the room. This EVP greeting has been recorded on tape recorders. When I heard it, I noted that the voice sounded like it belonged to a living person; it was sharp and clear, delivered in a man's modulated low tone. The guests of the MVD Ghostchasers who stayed in here heard knocking on the door throughout their stay. (Was it the room's friendly male ghost or that of Mary Darcy?)

Other rooms are haunted in their own, unique ways. Room 15 contains a female spirit who is quite friendly with male guests. She has been known to shake them or pull the linens from the bed. She has also been known to push female guests. Room 30's accommodations include a sweet-smelling perfume that sometimes filters through the air. Room 40 is filled by a high-energy field that causes equipment failures where, for example, new batteries die and cameras shut down. There have also been many EVP voices recorded here. Room 43 is inhabited by a male ghost whose loud snores have awakened many guests.

Mary Darcy has been known to make her rounds throughout the night, maintaining her hotel's wholesome reputation. Her ghost is apparently continuing this tradition of overseeing the nightly goings on at the Hotel Lee. Perhaps Mary knows that the magic of the old hotel still lingers through its ghostly guests.

Address:	390 South Main Street, Yuma, AZ 85364
Phone:	928-783-6336
Fax:	928-783-6336
Email:	linda@hotellee.com
Website:	www.hotellee.com
Contact:	Bob Glade and Linda Guess, owners
Lodging:	30 rooms, restaurant, coffee bar, shops
Amenities:	AC, cable, mini refrigerators, microwaves, bathrooms in hall, full bathrooms in suites

Ghost Hunter's Tools

AUDIO RECORDER–to record EVPs

BASIC FIRST AID KIT–just in case

BATTERIES–to keep all manner of ghost equipment running

CAMERAS–to detect visual anomalies: 3-5X digital, 35mm with high speed film (400 ASA), disposable cameras (400 ASA) and night vision camcorders

COMPASS–for picking up electromagnetic forces–a compass will react to any magnetic or electrical stimulus that is out of the ordinary (as well as showing you the way home)

CELL PHONE or **WALKIE-TALKIE**–for staying in touch when you are spread out

DOWSING ROD–Employed to locate hidden things using two L-shaped metal rods, one held in each hand parallel to the ground and to each other. When the dowser passes through anomalous energy, the rods will either swing apart or cross each other.

EMF METER–(Electromagnetic Field Meter) A device that measures levels of electromagnetic field changes in an area. A ghost's aura can generate distortions in the field, so where there are ghosts, there are generally significantly varied electromagnetic readings. The higher the reading, the more likely it is that paranormal activity is taking place.

FLASHLIGHTS–illumination for dark places

FILM–you can never have too much film or recording tape

MOTION DETECTOR–monitors unseen heat or object movement using infrared motion detection, picking up activity that would otherwise go unnoticed

NOTEBOOK and **PEN**–to log any phenomena seen, felt or experienced

TAPE MEASURE–for documenting location/event distances or dimensions

THERMAL SCANNER–infrared thermal scanners detect cold spots or other temperature fluctuations

WATCH–to record time phenomena occur

Ghost Hunter's Vocabulary

ANOMALY–Something found with no explainable source.

APPARITION–Any disembodied spirit that appears visibly to the naked eye or on film. It can be shadowy or take on a glowing, transparent form and sometimes appears without legs or feet. This is the rarest of photographable spirit phenomena.

COLD SPOT–An area characterized by a significant drop in temperature compared to the surrounding area (significant usually being a 25 degree or more difference). It is believed that a ghost uses the energy surrounding it to manifest itself and, in so doing, creates a cold air mass.

ECTO MISTS–Swirling, vaporous clouds of spirit matter.

ECTOPLASM–A solid or vaporous substance that smells like ozone, often white in appearance, but usually invisible to the naked eye. It looks like swirling clouds in a photo and at times takes the form of human faces, limbs or even entire bodies.

EVP–(Electronic Voice Phenomena) A recording on audiotape, videotape, film or a digital device for which there is no physical source. When the spirit voices are recorded, no sounds seem present but on playback, hushed voices can be heard. Most are difficult to understand.

GHOST–A form of apparition. The disembodied soul of a dead person believed to be an inhabitant of the unseen world that appears to the living in its former bodily likeness.

HAUNT–A ghost that returns to the same location on a recurring basis. Ghosts haunt places, not people.

HIGH-ENERGY AREA–A high-energy area will leave the hair on your arms standing on end! It is an area of significant paranormal activity. You will often get good photos and/or EVPs (and your camera batteries will often die quickly!).

ORB–The basic energy pattern of the spirit world and most commonly photographed spirit phenomenon. It is condensed energy and the easiest form in which spirits manifest. Orbs are various sizes and colors. They look like glowing bubbles of light on film and cannot usually be seen with the naked eye.

PARANORMAL–Something that is beyond the range of normal human experience or scientific explanation, i. e. supernatural.

VORTEX–Consists of dozens of orbs moving together at very high speeds. They appear as swirling columns of light.

Index

Index (continued)

Index (continued)

Ghost References

Ghost References (continued)

MVD Ghostchaser Team

Back Row (left to right): Stu, Gary, Liz, Denise, Debe, Kenton. *Middle Row (left to right):* Beth, Mollie, Shiela, Maddie. *Front Row (left to right):* Nicole, Chris, Nancy.

About the Author

Debe Branning

Debe Branning has been the director of the paranormal team, the MVD Ghostchasers, since 1995. She and her band of rowdy ghost hunters conduct regular investigations of haunted historic locations throughout Arizona. Debe also coordinates and organizes spirit workshops in various haunted establishments around the state. She has been interviewed on radio talk shows and featured in television news reports and special features about haunted sites, including an internationally broadcast special on Telemundo television about one of her favorite haunted hotels in Douglas, Arizona. The subject of several newspaper and magazine stories on ghost sightings, Debe has ghost-hunted with paranormal investigators across the country, including teams in Nebraska, Louisiana, Texas and Kentucky. When she's not ghost-hunting, she enjoys speaking about her experiences hunting for ghosts and is a regular guest speaker at Ottawa University on the subject of ghost photography and ghost hunting.

A native of Omaha, Nebraska, Debe has resided in Mesa, Arizona, for over 25 years. During this time, she has traveled to every corner of the state studying Arizona's history and culture, having great "normal" and paranormal adventures. In addition to traveling and writing, her hobbies include collecting celebrity dolls and old postcards, hiking and serving as an adult member of a Girl Scout troop. She is the proud parent of two children, Justin Hampton and Nicole Wheeler.

Debe is also the proud owner of a 1972 Cadillac Hearse named Sabrina.

Website: www.mvdghostchasers.iwarp.com
Email: NAZANAZA@aol.com

More Ghostly Adventures from Golden West Publishers

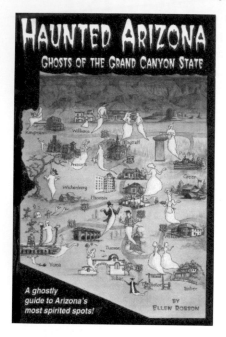

HAUNTED ARIZONA
Ghosts of the
Grand Canyon State

Witnesses at these haunted sites swear that the spirits of those who lived in Arizona's wild past are still among us. From ruthless outlaws to priests and Victorian ladies, these ghost stories will amaze you! By Ellen Robson, co-author of *Haunted Highway: The Spirits of Route 66*.

5 1/2 x 8 1/2 — 136 pages . . . $12.95

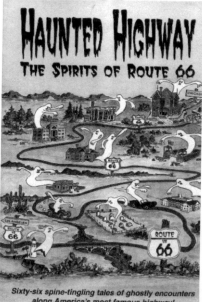

HAUNTED HIGHWAY:
The Spirits of Route 66

These fascinating accounts of ghostly activities will provide you with hours of reading enjoyment. Sixty-six spine-tingling tales of haunted homes, businesses and graveyards to be found along America's "Mother Road." From the *Biograph Theater* in Chicago to the *Pointe Vincente Lighthouse* on the Pacific Coast. Take a trip on Route 66 as the authors investigate and record stories of ghostly legends and actual ghost encounters. A great guide for the adventurous. By Ellen Robson and Dianne Halicki.

5 1/2 x 8 1/2—192 pages . . . $12.95

More books from Golden West Publishers

ARIZONA ADVENTURE

Daring deeds and exploits of Wyatt Earp, Buckey O'Neill, the Rough Riders, Arizona Rangers, and the notorious Tom Horn, to name a few. Read about the Power brothers shootout, Pleasant Valley wars, the Hopi revolt—action-packed true tales of early Arizona! By Marshall Trimble.

5 1/2 x 8 1/2 — 160 Pages . . .$9.95

ARIZONA LEGENDS & LORE

Stories of Southwestern pioneers by a master storyteller: *Mysterious Lady in Blue, Captivity of Olive Oatman, Dutchman's Gold, Vulture Gold, Sharlot Hall, Louisa Wetherill and the Navajos,* and more! By Dorothy Daniels Anderson.

5 1/2 x 8 1/2—176 pages . . . $9.95

Marshall Trimble's Official
ARIZONA TRIVIA

A fascinating book about Arizona! Arizona's master storyteller and humorist challenges trivia lovers with 1,000 questions on Arizona's people, places, politics, sports, cactus, geography, history, entertainment and much more!

5 1/2 x 8 1/2 — 176 Pages . . . $8.95

GHOST TOWNS
and Historical Haunts in Arizona

Visit cities of Arizona's golden past, browse through many photographs of adobe ruins, old mines, cemeteries, ghost towns, cabins and castles! Step into Arizona's past!

5 1/2 x 8 1/2—144 pages . . . $6.95

TALES OF ARIZONA TERRITORY

True stories of Arizona's pre-statehood history. Adventures and misadventures of pioneers, lawmen, desperadoes, stage coaches and stage stations. By Charles E. Lauer.

5 1/2 x 8 1/2 — 160 Pages . . . $9.95

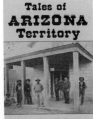

GOLDEN WEST PUBLISHERS

☼ 4113 N. Longview Ave. • Phoenix, AZ 85014
www.goldenwestpublishers.com • **1-800-658-5830** • FAX 602-279-6901

Qty	Title	Price	Amount
	Arizona Cook Book	6.95	
	Arizona Adventure	9.95	
	Arizona Legends and Lore	9.95	
	Arizona Trails & Tales	9.95	
	Arizona Trivia	8.95	
	Arizoniana	9.95	
	Arrows, Bullets & Saddle Sores	9.95	
	Discover Arizona!	6.95	
	Explore Arizona!	6.95	
	Ghost Towns in Arizona	6.95	
	Grand Canyon Cook Book	6.95	
	Haunted Arizona: Ghosts of the Grand Canyon State	12.95	
	Haunted Highway: The Spirits of Route 66	12.95	
	Hiking Arizona	6.95	
	Mimbres Mythology	19.95	
	Old West Adventures in Arizona	6.95	
	Scorpions & Venomous Insects of the SW	9.95	
	Sleeping With Ghosts: AZ Ghost Hunters Guide	12.95	
	Snakes and other Reptiles of the SW	9.95	
	Tales of Arizona Territory	9.95	
Shipping & Handling Add:	United States $4.00 Canada & Mexico $6.00—All others $13.00		

☐ My Check or Money Order Enclosed

☐ MasterCard ☐ VISA

Total $ _____

(Payable in U.S. funds)

Acct. No. _____ Exp. Date _____

Signature _____

Name _____ Phone _____

Address _____

City/State/Zip _____

Call for a FREE catalog of all of our titles

4/05 This order blank may be photocopied Sleeping with Ghosts